# POETICS OF UNDERGROUND SPACE

This book investigates the relationship architecture has with the underground. It provides a broad ranging historical and theoretical survey of, and critical reflection on, ideas pertaining to the creation and occupation of underground space. It overturns the classic dictates of construction on the surface and through numerous examples explores recoveries of existing voids, excavations, caves, quarries, grottos and burrows.

The exploitation of land, especially in areas of particular value, has given rise to the need to reformulate the usual approach to building. If the development of urban sprawl, its infrastructure and its networks, generates increasingly compromised landscapes, what are the possible strategies to transform, expand and change the usual relationship between abuse of soil and unused subsoil?

Psychological, philosophical, literary and cinematographic legacies of underground architecture are mixed with the compositional, typological and constructive expedients, to produce a rich, diverse and compelling argument for these spaces. As such, the book will appeal to architecture students, scholars and academics as well as those with an interest in literary theory, cinema and cultural studies.

**Antonello Boschi** (1964) studied in Florence, where he graduated with Adolfo Natalini and gained a Ph.D. in Architectural and Urban Design. His essays, works and reviews have been published in *Abitare, Area, Archi, Architécti, Arquitectura Viva, Bauwelt, Casabella, Detail, Diseño Interior, Interni, Materia, On Diseño, Rassegna, The Architectural Review.* Major writings include *Fenomenologia della facciata* (Milan 2010), *Ri-scritture/Re-Writings* (Milan 2011), *Filosofia del Nascosto. Costruire, pensare, abitare nel sottosuolo* (Venice 2015), *L'architettura della villa moderna* (Macerata 2016–2017–2018), *Abbandoni e resistenze. Note per una fenomenologia della facciata nel Novecento* (Pisa 2020). He is currently Associate Professor at the School of Engineering in Pisa, where he lectures on Architectural Composition.

# POETICS OF UNDERGROUND SPACE

## Architecture, Literature, Cinema

Antonello Boschi

Foreword by Michael Jakob

LONDON AND NEW YORK

First published 2022
by Routledge
2 Park Square, Milton Park, Abingdon, Oxon OX14 4RN

and by Routledge
605 Third Avenue, New York, NY 10158

*Routledge is an imprint of the Taylor & Francis Group, an informa business*

© 2022 Antonello Boschi

The right of Antonello Boschi to be identified as author of this work has been asserted by him in accordance with sections 77 and 78 of the Copyright, Designs and Patents Act 1988.

All rights reserved. No part of this book may be reprinted or reproduced or utilised in any form or by any electronic, mechanical, or other means, now known or hereafter invented, including photocopying and recording, or in any information storage or retrieval system, without permission in writing from the publishers.

*Trademark notice*: Product or corporate names may be trademarks or registered trademarks, and are used only for identification and explanation without intent to infringe.

*British Library Cataloguing-in-Publication Data*
A catalogue record for this book is available from the British Library

*Library of Congress Cataloging-in-Publication Data*
Names: Boschi, Antonello, 1964– author.
Title: Poetics of underground space / Antonello Boschi.
Description: Abingdon, Oxon ; New York : Routledge, 2022. |
Includes bibliographical references and index.
Identifiers: LCCN 2021017051 (print) | LCCN
2021017052 (ebook) | ISBN 9781032069920 (hardback) |
ISBN 9781032103624 (paperback) | ISBN 9781003214960 (ebook)
Subjects: LCSH: Underground architecture. | Underground areas.
Classification: LCC NA2542.7 .B67 2022 (print) |
LCC NA2542.7 (ebook) | DDC 720/.473—dc23
LC record available at https://lccn.loc.gov/2021017051
LC ebook record available at https://lccn.loc.gov/2021017052

ISBN: 978-1-032-06992-0 (hbk)
ISBN: 978-1-032-10362-4 (pbk)
ISBN: 978-1-003-21496-0 (ebk)

DOI: 10.4324/9781003214960

Typeset in Bembo
by codeMantra

Translations Steve Piccolo

Collaboration in bibliographic research Silvia Berti,
Maria Rita Macchi

This volume is dedicated to my wife Antonella and my son Jacopo

# CONTENTS

| | | |
|---|---|---|
| *Foreword* | | *ix* |
| 1 | Huddling | 1 |
| 2 | Notes from underground | 15 |
| 3 | The city other | 29 |
| 4 | Mimicry | 43 |
| 5 | Novelty is but oblivion | 56 |
| 6 | Stone skies | 67 |
| 7 | Sensations | 80 |
| 8 | Sous passages | 95 |
| 9 | Buried high-rises | 107 |

**viii** Contents

10  Brightening the dark                                         118
    *Antonello Boschi and Antonio Salvi*

*Bibliography*                                                   *133*
*Index*                                                          *141*

# FOREWORD

As inhabitants of a thin portion of the earth's upper crust, our customary vertical orientation implies an upward gaze. The "here" is thus defined in comparison to a beyond, which due to its character as a transcendent territory *par excellence* takes on a supremely positive value.

The world beneath our feet (far from the head), on the other hand, has a globally negative value. More complex and layered than the sky, more ambiguous because we imagine it as a source of extreme cold and heat, the *mundus subterraneus* generally remains not only invisible, but also scarcely explored.

On close inspection, the underground sphere represents a fascinating and important *other*. What lies hidden in the bowels of the earth is also, first of all, that which can never constitute a landscape. Because landscape emerges as a remnant of land and/or of nature thanks to the perceptive act of a subject. Therefore, when we talk about landscape an open space is immediately implied, a horizon, as well as freedom of movement. In the underground sphere this does not happen, and it is also for this reason that "down there" we feel lost, blocked, imprisoned. Of course there is also the anthropologically proven sensation of being wrapped and protected by what is not exposed to the light of day. The cavern, the lair, the grotto, the crypt, the architecture that extends below ground, undoubtedly have a "maternal" quality, acting as an enclosure that promises safety and primordial wellbeing. In the long run, this protective quality vanishes, and it is

**x** Foreword

only in myth or the collective imaginary that the underground world can survive with its status as a safe haven.

*To live* underground – even if we are in a large hidden city – remains psychologically and phenomenologically frustrating. The most congenial expression of this sensation appears in the last text written by Kafka: *Der Bau* (*The Burrow*). Before dying, imprisoned in his tuberculosis, Kafka described the complex subterranean world built by a badger-like creature. Conceived to provide the animal with symbolic physical and nutritional security, as well as a sense of prosperity ("There I sleep the sweet sleep of tranquility, of satisfied desire, of achieved ambition; for I possess a house"), the fact of having made a labyrinth of great complexity nevertheless remains an aporetic action, because the enemy *above* the creature's head is always lurking. Unlike Novalis, who was still able to glimpse the possibility of an existential regeneration through momentaneous immersion in the underground world, Kafka emphasizes the illusive nature of a lasting salvation in the depths of the earth. In this context, we should also obviously consider the historical situation and the transformation of the modern cognitive horizon. Novalis, a mining engineer and romantic poet, knew very well that the episode narrated in his *Heinrich von Ofterdingen* was simply a fantasy. In an era of underground construction of military infrastructures, tunnels, and then penstocks and power stations, the underground sphere was shaped by man in exactly the same way as the normally visible surface of the earth. From Romanticism onward (which coincides, we should not forget, with the industrial revolution), underground excursions would function only when they took on the short form of the epiphany. One goes down for a time in a katabasis, visiting Pompeii for example, and imagining everything that is still there to be dug up; or one descends together with archaeologists into the underground metropolis, with Fellini (*Roma*, 1972), to gaze upon a treasure that tragically vanishes if exposed to the danger (the air) of the everyday world. In a modern or postmodern regimen, the underground sphere thus acts as a reservoir of ideas and cultural immersions, of epiphanies in the name of difference. A sizeable quantity of what is seen as original is indeed born "underground," but this happens with the aim of its assertion up there, on the surface.

The erudite and richly illustrated essay by Antonello Boschi has the great virtue of enabling us to know what usually remains impalpable. He provides a mapping of the underground world, and he does so in an interdisciplinary way. The reminder that what lies "below" has to do with us is not, in this case, a mere dialectical exercise of style: never before as in our time, with its talk of (increasingly depleted) resources, has it been so

Foreword **xi**

urgent to realize that nearly all those resources exist below ground. Boschi's exegesis, in the end, is also a way of making us rethink architecture. The latter, on the one hand, is anchored in a system that exploits the underground world in all kinds of ways, and it is also true that architecture has never occupied as much underground space as it does today. On the other, with underground non-landscape space architecture shares the possibility of protecting us and isolating us from the outside world lurking in ambush. Architecture has always been lair, cavern, shelter, also and above all. So thinking about the underground means thinking about architecture.

Michael Jakob

# 1
# HUDDLING

The natural distrust of the subterranean world has distant, mysterious and deep roots. They are undoubtedly historical in character, because shelter has been an issue in every period of the past, at every latitude; but they are also cultural. While in the past going to ground was a way of surviving, of seeking protection from the elements, of choosing the earth as a roof under which to live rather than a surface on which to tread, with the advent of the industrial revolution the underground universe has coincided with the concept of mobility. The belly of Paris, as well as other capitals, began to contain not just immense sewer systems, but also entire underground rail lines.

In this way, the substrate has wound up taking on different forms and meanings: on the one hand, the contribution to public hygiene made by the Romans through the introduction of sewers and the Cryptoporticus (Figure 1.1), a true service tunnel, and on the other the pedestrian mobility of the capital of Canada and certain northern European cities[1]; just consider the use of underground spaces as water tanks or to store comestibles, and as parking areas in contrast with modern above-ground garage facilities. We can think about the importance assigned in the past to lodgings – whose term fully indicates the temporary nature of the construction, as opposed to the tombs and burials, considered *domus aeternae* – and how the latter tell us much more about certain civilizations than the remains of houses or huts.[2] Or we can consider the symbol that from Freud[3] onward fastens onto the dark thoughts of anyone who descends into the bowels of the earth (Figure 1.2):

> He was fascinated in particular by necropoli. […] He often visited them […] and immersed himself in that navel of earth that led him

DOI: 10.4324/9781003214960-1

**2** Huddling

**FIGURE 1.1** View of the Cryptoporticus, Aosta, 1st century BC © Antonello Boschi.

**FIGURE 1.2** Graciela Vilagudin, *Nude man in a hole in fetal position*, 2019 © Graciela Vilagudin.

Huddling  **3**

in front of a vagina-gate so precisely represented as to trigger the urge to sin. Through that gate one enters a uterus that grants death. […] To wedge oneself into the uterine tube and enter that warm, silent place, a place of life forever and therefore of death, one has to crouch and curl into the fetal position […] He liked to vanish from the surface of the earth and hide down there, in the mystery, inside the earth, becoming earth forever.[4] (Figure 1.3).

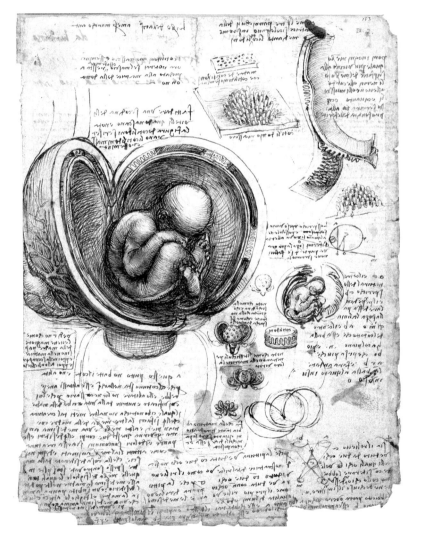

**FIGURE 1.3** Leonardo da Vinci, *The fetus in the womb*, 1510–1512 Royal Collection Trust © Her Majesty Queen Elisabeth II 2020.

## 4 Huddling

An image, that of the cryptal architecture, fed as can be seen by mythology, literature, comics and other expressions of a narrative character, like cinema. From the Chasm of Tartarus to Plato's cave, the *Commedia* of Dante to the *Mundus subterraneus* of Father Kircher (Figure 1.4), from *Gulliver's Travels* by Swift to the voyage of Niels Klim by Holberg, to Casanova and Poe,[5] the archetypal vortex of adventure continued to dig a path into the center of the earth, until a 19th-century writer was able to make his popular descent. We are reminded of one of the first "modern" science fiction accounts, the *Voyage dans la lune* of Cyrano de Bergerac that already contains, in embryonic form, the concept of mobile architecture, legitimizing the winter burial of lodgings in terms of climate. We can look at *The Castle of Otranto* by Horace Walpole, which in its story exploits all the effects of the underground pathway, the secret passage, mystery, darkness, or the crypt of the vampire that grants concrete representation in popular fantasy

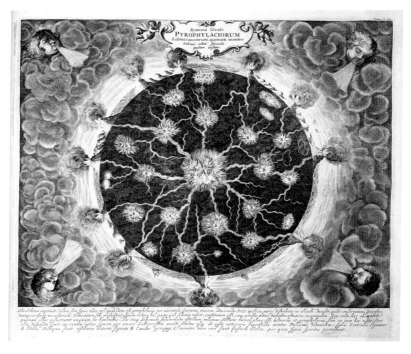

**FIGURE 1.4** Athanasius Kircher, *Systema Ideale Pyrophylaciorum Subterraneorum, quorum montes vulcanii, veluti spiracula quaedam existant*, Amsterdam 1665.

**FIGURE 1.5** Édouard Riou, *Ce n'est qu'une forêt de champignons*, illustration from *Voyage au centre de la terre*, by Jules Verne, Paris 1864.

to the mysteries of ancient labyrinths and the shrines of archaic or initiatic cults. In *The Time Machine* by Herbert George Wells the traveler discovers the existence of a community, the Morlocks, that lives in the darkness amidst the din of machinery and ventilation devices. We can talk about Jules Verne, who describes the *sous-sol* not only in his famous *Voyage* (Figure 1.5), but also in *Les Indes noires* where the protagonist, Simon Ford, raised in a coal mine, refuses to abandon that microcosm so arduously conquered.[6] Words that become images in the drawings and etchings of Abildgaard, Piranesi, Barbant, or in the scenes of the slaves in *Metropolis* by Fritz Lang (Figure 1.6), the outcasts hidden in the sewers in *Batman Returns* by Tim Burton and the poor of Kim family in *Parasite* by Bong Joon-ho (Figure 1.7).

The passage from literature to film cannot help but have repercussions on our way of looking downward: it is as if the underground had absorbed the sinister, anguishing traits, *Misérables*, of the hiding places of Hugo's hero Jean Valjean, and had transported them onto 35 mm celluloid. First going to occupy only the depths of manholes, passages and tunnels in *The*

**6** Huddling

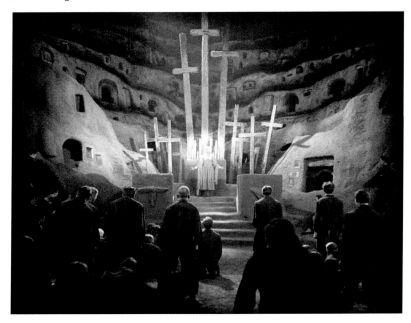

**FIGURE 1.6** Still taken from *Metropolis*, by Fritz Lang, Germany 1927.

**FIGURE 1.7** Still taken from *Parasite*, by Bong Joon-ho, South Korea 2019.

*Third Man* by Carol Reed, then the metro lines and parking areas that quickly become the preferred places for criminals: attacks, illegal dealings, chases, swapping of hostages – in short, the entire reservoir of images to which we have been accustomed by *noir*, thriller and espionage genres.

Therefore not just the magic of the Parisian voyage of *Zazie dans le métro*, the surreal characters of *Subway*, the outcasts of London in *Extreme Measures* or the theme of New York escape of *The Warriors*, but also the garages of *Someone to Watch Over Me* or *All the President's Men*. All the way to the extreme recipe of people relegated to an existence of suffering in the many conflicts, epidemics and dystopian scenarios of science fiction – *Things to Come*,[7] *THX 1138, Soylent Green*,[8] *Twelve Monkeys* – as well as fears more imaginary than real, as in *Blast from the Past* or *Underground*. And while the foundations of a building embody solidity, rationality, almost the memory, the echo of construction, a small space like a cellar can also become a metaphor of the unconscious (*The Spiral Staircase, A Nightmare on Elm Street, The Hole*, etc.).

Timeless images, shared mental landscapes that combined with much more concrete fears of attack could not fail to influence the approach to architectural design. While fear – physical or psychological – is what most people project onto any type of underground construction, linking back to images of darkness, filth, dampness, precisely the idea of a closed, hidden space, of which we speak reluctantly as we do of embarrassing relatives, could give rise to a noble "clandestine" architecture.

In the second half of the last century the problem shifted from the aesthetic of mobility, with its vehicular tunnels, pedestrian underpasses and underground rail lines, to the aesthetic of stable places like museums, convention halls and shopping centers, without overlooking residential architecture. But what has truly changed in the approach to the underground is the loss of symbolic content in favor of the mere resolution of problems of space. A passage from refuge to container, at the expense of what should be the design guidelines, such as cultural, perceptive and psychological implications. An often honest operation of civil engineering, as opposed to architectural identity, a forceful image and – as a result – clear recognizability: the sensation that often the work proceeds by subtraction[9] rather than positive addition, with that sense of bewilderment that the lack of characterization of underground spaces brings with it. Two very different examples can be of use here. Mumford thought these spaces wound up, to some extent, as reminders of the British mining culture of the Coketowns[10] or the French wartime construction of the Ligne Maginot or the Réduit of the Swiss Alps, and he even spoke of "premature burial," referring to the need for the presence of living human beings to control the subterranean city. On the other hand, there is the typical Italian urge to illegally transform the few square meters that were made to contain the garage of suburban houses into dens: places for convivial lunches and dinners (in the dark), "conserving" the parquet in the formal living area on the ground floor (lighted).

Where otherwise large margins of maneuver could exist, as in areas of limited traffic in historical centers, the proliferation of crafts complexes, shopping centers and the entire range of containers that have almost no industrial character, where it would be possible to minimize the impact on the territory by literally burying the content, this is not done because it would limit external visibility – meaning advertising, and meaning income. There have been intermediate attempts, such as the Vulcano Buono in Nola (Figure 1.8),[11] which nevertheless conserve the aura of an open-air dump, those improbable hills that stand out against the flatness of the countryside, indicated by the swarming of cars in the outdoor parking areas, exactly like the circling of seagulls in search of food. The exact opposite of a visionary – but not too much – project by Zanuso for the caverns of Naples, where the building is grafted into the area of the Vallone without any Arcadian or pre-industrial posturing, and literally opening at the walls produces flowers, vegetables, in a word: nature.[12]

**FIGURE 1.8** Aerial view of the *Vulcano Buono* shopping mall by Renzo Piano Building Workshop, Nola 2007 © Moreno Maggi courtesy RPBW.

Huddling **9**

The rules of superficial (rather than surface) architecture thus continue to be applied, relying on the farsightedness of clients or the sensitivity of architects. The evolution of construction techniques has made it possible to artificially recreate the theme of the shelter, but the problem still remains that of the character of the building, that character that has always represented the *trait d'union* between the activities performed inside a construction and its external legibility, between content and container, which cannot help but reach a crisis in a work of architecture without facades.

From a certain period onward, telluric buildings – like their aboveground counterparts – have been based on the idea of a multifunctional container, theoretically capable of changing its skin to adapt to different uses and situations. It is easy to foresee further possible expansions of underground areas, plausible connections with other structures, all operations that are necessarily part of urban planning. Spaces that can from time to time host different functions, often with aberrant results, pertain to another line of discourse. What should be a forcefully characterized habitat winds up combining architectural anonymity with the sense of disorientation caused by the lack of contact with the outside world and with nature, in particular. While certain cities have avoided this tunnel effect by designing layouts that perfectly match the external circulation network, thus granting immediate recognizability to pathways – with the term "subway," below the way, as opposed to the more generic "underground" – the schemes of many structures can also replicate the above-ground plan, transforming volumes into parallel subterranean buildings.

If this can somehow increase the familiarity of immersion in the ground, we might hypothesize that the contradiction lines essentially in the plan, the axes, the nodes, routes and meeting points. But this is not the only compositional issue: cavern, crypt, grotto are all synonyms for a theme that investigates the relationship architecture continues to weave with the surface, the lighting and arrangement of internal spaces, which marks the reversal of the value of the enclosure. Here, in fact, the external skin becomes pure interior, the full becomes empty, overturning the classic dictates of construction on the ground: some are recoveries of existing voids, others excavate, cut, penetrate the rock, others still shape the roof in a "naturally" artificial way. But they all share the search for a sunbeam that breaks through the darkness that always cloaks these inhabited spaces, not just in the physical sense.

Hence many scholars have hastened to underline the role of curved shapes and level shifts along pathways,[13] the positioning of greenery and gathering points,[14] the great importance of visual examination of the spaces found along the way,[15] or – when design quality is lacking – how the commercial spaces wind up being characterized by a jumble of overlapping advertising messages.[16]

At times these places are true puzzles, mazes, labyrinths, like that of the Wieliczka salt mine (Figure 1.9), admirably described by the English traveler Stephen Jones, after a descent into the underworld by means of rope hoists:

> a kind of subterraneous republic. [...] This is wholly scooped out of one vast bed of salt, which is all a hard rock, as bright and glittering as crystal, and the whole space before him is formed of lofty arched vaults, supported by columns of salt, and roofed and floored with the same, so that the columns, and indeed the whole fabric, seem composed of the purest crystal.[17]

A place without windows, capable of marking the triumph of "*Das Licht will durch das ganze All / Und ist lebendig im Kristall*"[18] – in keeping with Scheerbart's maxim – could not but be a material exception. It is the section that makes movement and pause in an underground place a true sensorial experience, permitting the mixture of aspects of respect, symbiosis with

FIGURE 1.9  Jules Rocault, *Vue des travaux souterrains dans les mines de sel de Wieliczka, en Gallicie*, illustration from, *Les merveilles de l'industrie ou description des principales industries modernes* by Louis Figuier, Paris 1873.

nature, insertion in the context, with the forceful, allegorical, rooted idea of the shelter, of geological habitation. And it is light that reveals the section and generates the spaces: the *Piscina Mirabilis* (Figures 1.10 and 1.11) would not be the same without the sunlight arriving from the upper wells to bring out the pillars and arcades; the entrance to the Cumaean Sibyl's Cave would

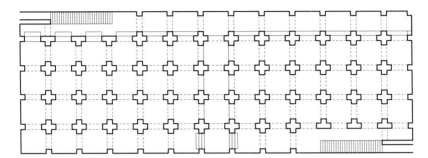

**FIGURE 1.10** Plan of the *Piscina Mirabilis*, Bacoli, 27 BC–14 AD.

**FIGURE 1.11** View of the hall © Antonello Boschi.

## 12 Huddling

be only a narrow passage – in spite of its trapezoidal profile – without the large openings towards the sea that accompany the path; the Treasure Museum of San Lorenzo would not have that diffused mystical glow – symbolically emphasized by the spokes of reinforced concrete – without Albini's apt intuition of the oculus that brightens the *tholos* (Figure 1.12). Hence the openings, the cuts, the contrast of luminosity and darkness are the factors that reduce the sense of oppression caused by the limited height of the spaces (Figure 1.13).

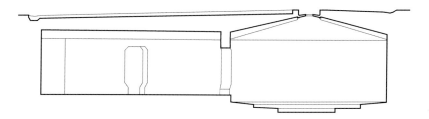

**FIGURE 1.12** Franco Albini, section of the Treasure Museum of San Lorenzo, Genoa 1956.

**FIGURE 1.13** Franco Albini, interior view of a room in the Treasure Museum of San Lorenzo, Genoa 2015 © Pietro Savorelli.

At first we cannot see beyond the path that leads downward to dark and hateful things – but no light or beauty will ever come from the man who cannot bear this sight. Light is always born of darkness, and the sun never yet stood still in heaven to satisfy man's longing or to still his fears.[19]

Only by gauging these elements can we prevent that sort of "zero shadow" effect, that sensation of immateriality that certain places end up having, which makes everything inevitably flat, monotonous, two-dimensional. Instead, we can obtain countless variations of natural light, the range of light temperatures of the sky, the sequence of the seasons, the sense of time passing.

Using glass partitions between spaces, ceilings higher than average and always proportioned to the footprint; inserting intersections, staggered levels, the creation of two-story volumes; placing connection lobbies between the ground and the underground to boost the sense of contact with the outside world and the capacity to perceive the form and measurements of the building. These are just a few of the many compositional expedients[20] that can erase the "'semantic noise' that prevents us from correctly evaluating the true meaning of immersion in the ground."[21]

The issue, then, is not to have a timid or simply low-profile attitude, but to have sensitivity, because speaking softly while avoiding unruly gestures is not an operation anyone can effectively perform. Nevertheless, it is only in this way that the umpteenth *Journey to the Center of the Earth* can again convey an enormous sensation of being "on the surface."[22]

## Notes

1  Generally one thinks of cities like Montreal, Toronto, Calgary, or Helsinki in Europe, where the problem is that of low annual average temperatures; but we should also consider very warm places like Houston, where a part of the population crosses the city protected from the sunlight, while the other people walk in the open air.

2  Bernard Rudofsky, *The Prodigious Builders: Notes Toward a Natural History of Architecture with Special Regard to those Species that are Traditionally Neglected or Downright Ignored* (New York: Harcourt Brace Jovanovich, 1977), 159–160.

3  "Dwellings were a substitute for the mother's womb, that first abode, in which he was safe and felt so content, for which he probably yearns ever after." Sigmund Freud, *Civilization and Its Discontents* (Mineola, NY: Dover Publications 1994), 23.

4  Vittorino Andreoli, *Fuga dal mondo* (Milan: Rizzoli, 2009), 158.

5  See Wendy Lesser, *The Life below the Ground. A Study of the Subterranean in Literature and History* (Winchester, MA: Faber and Faber, 1987).

**14** Huddling

6 Alberto Arecchi, "Il mondo sotterraneo nella letteratura," in *La casa nella Roccia. Architetture scavate e scolpite* (Milan: Mimesis, 2001), 153–162.

7 Dietrich Neumann, *Film Architecture: Set Designs from Metropolis to Blade Runner* (Munich: Prestel, 1999).

8 Aaron Betsky, "Introduction," in *Landscrapers: Building with the Land* (London: Thames & Hudson, 2002), 4–13.

9 See Sergio Polano, "L'architettura della sottrazione," *Casabella* 659 (September 1998): 2.

10 Lewis Mumford, *The City in History. Its Origins, Its Transformations and Its Prospects* (New York: Harcourt, Brace & World, 1961), 479–480.

11 See Antonello Boschi, "Architettura en travesti: mimetismi, camuffamenti e altri espedienti urbani," in Antonello Boschi, and Andrea Bulleri, *Suture(s)* (Pisa: Pacini, 2011), 40–45.

12 See Francesco Trabucco, "La fabbrica dei fiori. Un progetto di Marco Zanuso per l'area del Vallone San Rocco a Napoli, 1988," *Rassegna* 87 (June 2007): 54–63.

13 Naoji Matsumoto, Eiji Koyanagi, and Sigeyuki Seta, "Physical and Mental Factors of Anticipation in the Streetscape," in *Proceedings of the International Conference on Environment-Behavior Studies for the 21th Century* (Tokyo: 1997), 283–286.

14 Harmen Oppewal, and Harry Timmermans, "Modeling Consumer Perception of Public Space in Shopping Centers," *Environmental and Behavior* 31 (January 1999): 45–65.

15 John Zacharias, "Choosing a Path in the Underground: Visual Information and Preference," in *Proceedings of the 9th International Conference ACUUS Urban Underground Space a Resource for Cities* (Turin: ACUUS, 2002), 1–9.

16 Pierre Bélanger, "Underground Landscape: The Urbanism and the Infrastructure of Toronto's Downtown Pedestrian Network," *Tunnelling and Underground Space Technology* 22 (October 2006): 272–292.

17 Stephen Jones, *The History of Poland: From Its Origin as a Nation to the Commencement of the Year 1795. To Which Is Prefixed an Accurate Account of the Geography and Government of That Country and the Customs and Manners of Its Inhabitants* (London: Vernor & Hood, 1795), 30.

18 Paul Scheerbart, letter to Bruno Taut dated February 10, 1914, then in "Glasshausbriefe," *Frühlicht* 3 (February 1920): 45. "Light seeks to penetrate the whole cosmos / and is alive in Crystal."

19 Carl Gustav Jung, "The Spiritual Problem of Modern Man," in *Modern Man in Search of a Soul* (London: Routledge, 2001), 220.

20 In the flourishing manuals see Federica Avanza, Stefano Calchi Novati, and Simone De Munari, *Progettare il sottosuolo: elementi di cultura tecnica per l'architettura sotterranea* (Milan: FrancoAngeli, 1991) and John Carmody, and Raymond L. Sterling, *Underground Space Design. A Guide to Subsurface Utilization and Design for People in Underground Spaces* (New York: Van Nostrand Reinhold, 1993).

21 Giovanni Klaus Koenig, "Immersi nel terreno," *Ottagono* 74 (September 1984): 18.

22 Jules Verne, *Journey to the Centre of the Earth* (London: Puffin, 1994), 290.

# 2
# NOTES FROM UNDERGROUND

Just a few months passed between the opening of the London Underground (Figure 2.1) and the publication of Dostoevsky's *Notes from Underground*. Separated in terms of geography and culture, these events are nevertheless linked by the thin red thread of a "deep" change with respect to the works that preceded them. While the "Tube" and, more generally, the sections of the tunnels crossing major cities and capitals have altered the behavior and movements of inhabitants over the last 150 years, the novel by the Russian author changed the *modus operandi* of narration (Figure 2.2), shifting from a focus on the setting of the experience of the protagonist in a given habitat or a given era to an inner dimension that cast its influence on the entire 20th century. A protagonist that is not a social personality, but uses the underground as a metaphor, the image of digging into the human spirit, the unconscious,[1] what Jung defines as the "basements" of the soul, to mix it with the place from which his voice materially arrives.

If the use of transport in tunnels has been facilitated by continual and constant improvements to the individual segments in which the passenger travels, the matter differs when the distances oblige contact and dialogue with others. The *Chemin de fer métropolitain* is a good example, in this regard:

> When the trip takes a little longer than usual [...] they are less tolerant of the gaze of others and dare less to look at them; voyeurism takes its distance: parallel to the tracks, however, the windows of

DOI: 10.4324/9781003214960-2

16   Notes from underground

**FIGURE 2.1**   Kell Brothers, *Metropolitan Railway, Baker Street Station*, 1863 © Science Museum/Science & Society Picture Library.

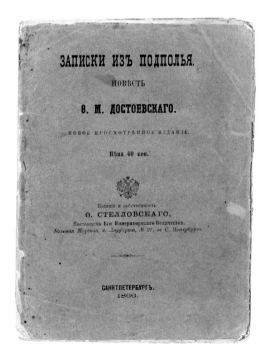

**FIGURE 2.2**   Fyodor Dostoevsky, *Zapiski iz podpol'ja. Povest*, Saint Petersburg 1866.

the apartment buildings on the third and fourth floors are often closed and the curtains drawn, as if the happy inhabitants of these places were obliged to 'play subway' at home and the whole day long to enjoy the quietude of a padded room in which the light is always on. Some people, more extroverted, more astute, or simply higher up, lean on their elbows at the window and watch the subways go by, the way others watch trains or cars from highway footbridges.[2]

For a "place of solitude, in which people avoid each other and glances are fleeting,"[3] paradoxically there exist different ways of looking "down." Gazes that are cross-eyed or at times incoherent, often mutable: social gazes, if we consider the metamorphosis of the basement in English-speaking countries, once the realm of the servants, accessed from the outside only by tradesmen, but now an integral part of the home; redeeming gazes, such as those exchanged in the air raid shelters of World War II, but also the anguished, doomed, claustrophobic gazes of fallout shelters, in America in the 1950s; and finally the imagined, ageless gazes, with Aeneas who ventures into the underworld of the dead, Virgil who acts as Dante's guide, Homer who ideally accompanies Schliemann through the territories of mythology and lands of archaeology.[4]

The caverns of ancient Greece through which one could descend into the afterworld had become the reality of the French tunnels:

> Our waking existence likewise is a land which, at certain hidden points, leads down into the underworld – a land full of inconspicuous places from which dreams arise. All day long, suspecting nothing, we pass them by, but no sooner has sleep come than we are eagerly groping our way back to lose ourselves in the dark corridors. […] This labyrinth harbors in its interior not one but a dozen blind raging bulls, into whose jaws not one Theban virgin once a year but thousands of anemic young dressmakers and drowsy clerks every morning must hurl themselves.[5]

And if the red signs in Paris indicated the modern route into Hades (Figure 2.3), the locomotives on the other side of the Channel came directly from the Vulcan's forge, evoking the divinities of the classical era: Pluto, Cerberus, Dido.

Cave of the gods in the classical, late antique and Christian tradition, the epic of the cavern is enriched by the legends of Tannhäuser or Wretched

## 18 Notes from underground

**FIGURE 2.3** Eugène Delacroix, *Dante and Virgil in Hell*, 1822 © RMN – Gran Palais (Musée du Louvre)/Franck Raux.

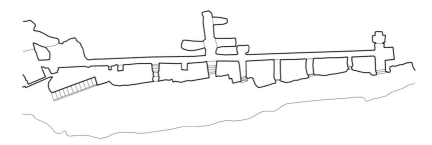

**FIGURE 2.4** Plan of the Sibyl's Cave, Cuma VII–VI century BC.

Guerrin in the Cave of the Sibyl (Figures 2.4 and 2.5), and the accounts of Lorenzo the Magnificent of the grottos of Pale. These traditions share the initial idea of a burial place, and later became the very image of darkness, the realm of mystery, the main dwelling place of our fears, a cosmos in which to venture with hesitancy and bewilderment.

**FIGURE 2.5** The trapezoidal section cut into the volcanic stone © Antonello Boschi.

But there is a difference between a rapid glance, "keeping one's eyes to oneself," and the lengthy roaming of the *flâneur* in underground spaces capable of causing discomfort and, in the worst cases, a true threat to physical and mental health. Extensive scientific literature exists regarding the appearance of problems of eyesight, migraines, common colds, fatigue and, more generally, conditions of stress in people who spend much of their time in underground work facilities: the main causes are humidity, lack of natural light, lack of air or sufficient air quality, accompanied by symptoms of fatigue that promptly arise due to lower levels of melatonin and cortisol.[6] These phenomena have been studied through laboratory research, but also tested in the field, in trials of on-site endurance over long periods of time. The experimentation with total isolation of Michel Siffre, starting in 1962 at Scarason in the Italian-French Maritime Alps, and ten years later at Midnight Cave in Texas, focused on the physical-psychological aspect, while the group headed by Maurizio Montalbini for the Biomedical Space Research Institute of NASA took a behavioral approach in Carlsbad

Caverns National Park, New Mexico.[7] At the outset the experiments were based on the possible physical repercussions on the human body, the more strictly physiological aspect of survival – a term utilized not by chance to underline the salvific yearning to return to the surface: staying underground implies a reduction or even a lack of sensory stimuli, a sort of blurring of sight, blunted hearing, neutralization of the sense of smell. In the darkness we lose the sense of where we are, of the passage of time and seasons. Under the ground, external sounds are muffled, while odors practically lose their force. And if this is true in relative terms, it is even truer in absolute ones, with sensations of temperature and humidity that become stable as compared to those outside. The only smells are those produced by our own body, the only sounds those caused by our steps, our movements, our voice. Above all, the light – when there is any – is often artificial, uniform in color temperature and intensity.[8]

If, as we have said, a series of images exists that inevitably crowd its way into the minds of architects – first of all the etchings of imaginary prisons by Piranesi (Figure 2.6), in which the sections reveal the classifying

**FIGURE 2.6** Giovanni Battista Piranesi, *Imaginary Prisons*, 1761.

precision of an entomologist – those same images perfectly embody our anxieties and illustrate thoughts that are not those of engineers, thoughts that have little to do with rationality. Almost a conditioned reflex capable of personifying not just the gloomy Dickensian figurations of the civilization of the steam-driven machine,[9] but also the real fears of miners, of people who have spent their whole lives under ground[10] in constant contact with the danger of *grisou*, the fear of collapses, admirably described by a writer-physician like Archibald Joseph Cronin.[11] The graphic approach and impressions raised in the observer differ in the sketches of Schinkel for the Cordari cave in Syracuse in his *Voyage in Sicily* or the drawings for the project of the Orianda Palace in Crimea (Figure 2.7), always described in positive terms: in the first, he comments on "the lush vegetation of fig trees and smallage at the entrance, through which the daylight shines,"[12] while for the second, he remarks on the attempt to create an interior "by treating its spaces as a cool promenade in a grotto."[13]

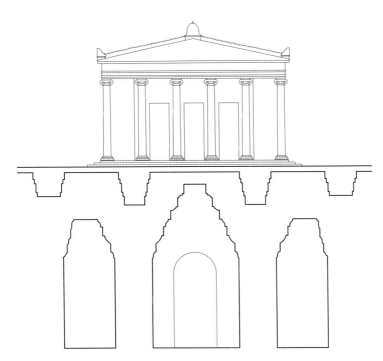

**FIGURE 2.7** Section of the *Project pour le musée de la Crimée et des provinces caucasiennes dans le château d'Orianda* by Karl Friedrich Schinkel, 1838.

## 22 Notes from underground

The unsuspected depth that lurks on the lower levels is a phenomenon not only telluric but also psychological in nature. The excellent example provided by Bachelard on the roof-cellar dichotomy may be of use here. Fundamentally, the basement level of a building can be seen as the simplest form of underground construction after the age of caverns. The roof embodies rationality (Figure 2.8), its slope indicates the climate conditions of the house; the roof cuts into the clouds, and it is there that the clearest ideas arise; the cellar too has its advantages and comforts (Figure 2.9) but it essentially personifies

> the *dark entity* of the house, the one that partakes of subterranean forces. When we dream there, we are in harmony with the irrationality of the depths. [...] The dreamer constructs and reconstructs the upper stories [...] but for the cellar, the impassioned inhabitant digs and re-digs, making its very depth active. The fact is not enough, the dream is at work. When it comes to excavated ground, dreams have no limit.[14]

We think of the dangers of the underground and describe them, above all, with the adjective ancestral, indicating something primordial, atavistic, although on its own it does not explain the belonging to the realm of the

**FIGURE 2.8** An attic © Antonello Boschi.

**FIGURE 2.9**  A cellar © Antonello Boschi.

imagination. And it is Jung, once more, through the image of the cellar and the attic, who indicates the fears that grip the human being: a dual nature of man, of the house and as a result of the terrain, which ends up materializing those natural fears as the irrational, madness, drama. Behind the wall in the attic there will always be light, while behind the walls of the basement there will be earth, earth and more earth.

A world can suggest sensations of trust, everyday familiarity, but also uncertainty, old and new misgivings. Trust obviously comes from the sense of protection embodied by the archetype of the cave, a drive towards adventure,[15] a place of concentration, elating and reassuring at the same time. The anxieties, instead, vary depending on the time of existence of the structures: we have seen that in all underground rail systems, especially if the trip is a short one, the individual is prompted to sublimate the sense of anguish through small expedients, such as lowering the gaze or riveting the eyes on reading matter, while the unavoidable negative thoughts remain, lurking in the back of the mind. Just observe the expressions of passengers when the train stops, even for a few dozen seconds, in a stretch of tunnel between two stations (Figure 2.10). In a crescendo, unspeakable and recurring fears undermine our certainties: the fear of a madman who can push

**24** Notes from underground

**FIGURE 2.10** *A woman walks through a heavily graffitied subway*, New York 1981 © Christopher Morris.

us onto the tracks from the platform, the nightmare of a terrorist attack – chemicals, explosives, bacteria – or a rail disaster, ever since the fire of 1903 in the Couronnes station, with a death toll of 84. When we shift from spaces of transit like tunnels, underpasses or parking garages towards others that call for limited stays, such as fitness clubs, restaurants, cinemas and shopping malls, or involve long-term presence, such as the territories of work and habitation, not only sensations of disorientation threaten our convictions.

Various researches have demonstrated that mystery, the hidden unknown, need not always be seen as negative factors, but can also be ways to make spaces and pathways more interesting and livable. Starting in the mid-1970s, the theories on landscape of Appleton, Kaplan and Kaplan shifted towards buildings and, in particular, shopping malls. The latter – chosen not only due to their exponential growth in number, but also as the most popular buildings in urban areas, offering a wide range of functions including shopping, eating, socializing, etc. – have been analyzed by photographing pathways and shoppers in different usage conditions. The results showed that mystery and appeal went together in the choice of the images, and how – in particular – the more complex the structure, marked by "multiple levels, well-defined spaces, pools of light, rich textures and warm colors,"[16] the greater its ability to attract. Now one might think that this research has been influenced by the geographical location, and this is true not so much due to a question of latitude as in terms of the cultural and ethnic make-up of the places.[17] Therefore the reactions change in Nordic countries – where starting in the 1970s various "artificial caverns" have been created to diminish pressures on land use, positioning swimming pools, fitness centers, theaters, but also offices, meeting rooms and even factories in these facilities – and where it has been noted that the lack of windows was compensated by human contact, and by the variety and size of the spaces. Isolated working positions, then, should be avoided because they can have such an impact on individuals that they perceive non-existent malfunctioning in the climate control systems, even when they are functioning perfectly.[18] In the United States the situation is more varied: in the interviews, the complaints are almost constant, but where the operation involves much greater depths than in traditionally "superficial" projects – as in the limestone mines of Kansas City (Figure 2.11) – the behavior of the people interviewed had some positive aspects. They expressed favorable views regarding factors like temperature and humidity with respect to the outside world, and above all the typical virtues and faults of the underground world were pushed aside by the vast size of the available spaces.[19] In China,

**FIGURE 2.11** Fords stored underground at *Subtropolis*, Kansas City, 1970 © Photo Courtesy of Hunt Midwest.

**26** Notes from underground

conduits and tunnels have been made under cities above all for defensive purposes, but where the quality of the air and lighting were not comparable to western standards, the poor conditions led to health problems, as well as fears of fire, flooding, earthquakes and structural collapse.[20] Negative thoughts that in Japan are transformed into types of anxiety regarding air quality, lack of awareness of the passing of time, and a sense of oppression. Significant experiments in this regard have been conducted in controlled conditions, comparing the working performance of individuals in areas with light from windows to that of other workers stationed in basements without particular corrective measures, or people working underground but aided by the presence of systems to capture natural light, the presence of trees and plants, monitors, and so on. The interesting factor, which confirms the importance of natural and direct light, is that at the outset the levels of assessment of these situations were practically equal, while over time the subjects having a window reported feeling more relaxed than the others. Furthermore, the best results in terms of work performance were reported when the passage to the depths of the earth happened by elevator, rather than by using a staircase.[21]

If every underground project is an excavation in depth – not only physical, but also symbolic depth – and if crevices, recesses, cavities and hollows are eroded spaces in which our weaknesses are materially laid bare, building, thinking about and inhabiting the underground wind up all becoming fragments of a philosophy of the hidden:

> a building whose upper story was erected in the nineteenth century, the ground floor dates back to the sixteenth century, and careful examination of the masonry reveals that it was reconstructed from a tower built in the eleventh century. In the cellar we come upon Roman foundations, and under the cellar a choked-up cave with Neolithic tools in the upper level and remnants of fauna from the same period in the low layers. That would be the picture of our psychic structure. We live on the upper story and are only aware that the lower story is slightly old-fashioned. As to what lies beneath the earth's surface, of that we remain totally unconscious.[22]

## Notes

1 Aldo Carotenuto, *I sotterranei dell'anima. Tra i mostri della follia e gli dèi della creazione* (Milan: Bompiani, 2008), 15–16.
2 Marc Augé, *In the metro* (Minneapolis: University of Minnesota Press, 2002), 54–55.

Notes from underground **27**

3 Ibid., "La complessità del sottosuolo," *La Repubblica*, October 23, 2006.
4 Freud often used archaeology as a metaphor to illustrate the very modalities of proceeding in the psychoanalytic method.
5 Walter Benjamin, *The Arcades Project*, ed. Rolf Tiedemann (Cambridge, MA: Belknap Press, 1999), 84.
6 Maria Luisa Cristina, Martina Sartini, and Paolo Orlando, "Caratteristiche ambientali degli spazi ipogei e benessere dei fruitori," in Angelo Bugatti, *Progettare il sottosuolo nella città densa e nel paesaggio*, ed. Ioanni Delsante (Santarcangelo di Romagna, RN: Maggioli, 2010), 31–40.
7 Maurizio Montalbini, "Stazioni ipogee. Esperimenti per un habitat possibile," *Rassegna* 87 (June 2007): 126–133.
8 In the months of March and April 2021, the *Deep Time* scientific mission tested the survival conditions of a group of seven men and seven women in the French caves of Lombrives at −12°C and with 95% humidity for a duration of forty days. Purpose of the experiment, promoted by the Human Adaptation Institute, is to verify the cognitive, epigenetic and physiological adaptation to new constraints, such as absence of light and lack of sense of the passing of time.
9 "The streets were hot and dusty on the summer day, and the sun was so bright that it even shone through the heavy vapour drooping over Coketown, and could not be looked at steadily. Stokers emerged from low underground doorways into factory yards, and sat on steps, and posts, and palings, wiping their swarthy visages, and contemplating coals." Charles Dickens, *Hard Times. For These Times* (Cambridge, MA: Riverside Press, 1869), 149.
10 One thinks of Hans Hollein who comes from a miners family and sees the subsoil not as a construction but as a real excavation. See Dietmar Steiner, "Sub-architecture: Dietmar Steiner interviews Hans Hollein," *Domus* 812 (February 1999): 4–6.
11 Archibald Joseph Cronin, *The Stars Look Down* (Boston, MA: Little, Brown and company, 1963), 182–207.
12 Karl Friedrich Schinkel, *Viaggio in Sicilia*, eds. Michele Cometa, and Gottfried Riemann (Messina: Sicania, 1990), 88.
13 Karl Friedrich Schinkel, "Letter of Schinkel to Tsarina Alexandra Feodorovna," in Klaus Jan Philipp, *Karl Friedrich Schinkel, Späte Projekte Late projects* (Stuttgart and London: Axel Menges, 2000), 1:114–115.
14 Gaston Bachelard, *The Poetics of Space* (Boston, MA: Beacon Press, 1969), 18.
15 A typical example of this form of optimism, it is a *Bildungsroman* like *The Adventures of Tom Sawyer*, where the little protagonist cannot but go on and where the entry and exit of this fantasy world don't coincide. Lesser, *The Life below the Ground*, 156–157, 166.
16 Richard Kent, "The Role of Mystery in Preferences for Shopping Malls," *Landscape Journal* 1 (March 1989): 28–35.
17 John Carmody, "Psychological and Physiological Effects in Underground Space," in Carmody, and Sterling, *Underground Space Design*, 137–152.
18 Jaakko Ylinen, "Architectural Design, Spatial Planning," in *The Rock Engineering Alternative*, ed. Kari Saari (Helsinki: Finnish Tunnelling Association, 1988), 77–88.
19 Joseph Hughey, and Robert Tye, "Psychological Reactions to Working Underground: A Study of Attitudes, Beliefs and Evaluations," *Underground Space* 5–6 (1983): 381–386.

**28** Notes from underground

20  Hou Xueyuan, and Yu Su, "The Urban Underground Space Environment and Human Performance," *Tunnelling and Underground Space Technology* 2 (1988): 193–200.
21  Yuji Wada, and Hinako Sakugawa, "Psychological Effects of Working Underground," *Tunnelling and Underground Space Technology* 1–2 (1990): 33–37.
22  Carl Gustav Jung, *The Earth Has a Soul: The Nature Writings of C.G. Jung*, ed. Meredith Sabini (Berkeley, CA: North Atlantic Books, 2002), 68.

# 3
# THE CITY OTHER

When we think about a city that is vanishing, a dying city, we always think of a place in a state of decay, where the inhabitants are gradually disappearing, or where the architecture has crumbled in time, destroyed by weathering and neglect. On the one hand, there is an almost surreal vanishing, where people abandon the city in search of new horizons and hopes, or to escape from poverty and natural catastrophes; on the other, we see a physical disappearance,[1] as indeed took place in the civilizations of the past, when sieges ended in the destruction of the settlement and the subsequent spreading of salt upon the ruins, to ward off resurgence from the ashes (Figure 3.1).[2]

Alongside Laudomia, which "too, will disappear, no telling when, and all its citizens with it," alongside Zora that "has languished, disintegrated, disappeared,"[3] there exists, however, another type of settlement that dissolves and does so quite willingly, seeking space in the folds of the underground; and this is the city that conceals itself, that will not let itself be seen, the camouflaged city.[4] A settlement that is perhaps seeking an outlet elsewhere, precisely when the planet – as Utudjian prophetically hypothesized in the 1930s – is in the meantime becoming too small for its ten billion inhabitants.[5] Utopian, visionary images, often apocalyptic perhaps, but in the end not so far from reality: there has been a passage from the design of structures for defensive purposes, such as the second Manhattan of Oscar Newman or the silos of the Cold War, to the project for the recovery of a diamond mine in Yakutia by Nikolay Lyutomskiy for Eco-City, or the

DOI: 10.4324/9781003214960-3

**30** The city other

**FIGURE 3.1** Aerial view of the ruins of the city, Carthage 1950 © Bertrand Boret.

wired city of *The Line* in the Saudi Arabia, which bears witness to the shift from a primordial underground era to the golden subterranean age.

What has changed between the realities of the past and modern, above all contemporary realities, is the design approach and the dimension of the projects. Before, there is the provisional or long-term occupation of the cave as refuge, as spontaneous architecture and – in the most complex cases – a sort of gemmation of contiguous spaces; after, there are clearly precise pathways, double volumes, crossed views, strategic openings to the outside, all envisioned, imagined, designed. From the mere reuse of existing places, or the implementation of a sum of works and interventions only subsequently capable of giving rise to a system, the approach passes to an "urban" idea of underground space. A conscious attitude, partially due to the evolution of excavation techniques (Figures 3.2 and 3.3), certainly the result of improvement of construction technologies (Figure 3.4), the development of natural and artificial lighting systems, the perfecting of ventilation equipment, but mainly produced by the awareness of a now-achieved normality of this type of intervention. Size has evolved in step with all this, passing from a troglodytic operation, so to speak, which as such sets its limits in the natural universe, to a process that transposes the modes of implementation of traditional urban planning into an underground key.

The city other 31

FIGURE 3.2   Alphonse de Neuville, *Les mineurs abattant le charbon*, illustration from *Le Creusot et les mines de Saone-et-Loire*, by Louis Laurent Simonin, Paris 1865 © Getty Images.

FIGURE 3.3   *Machine perforatrice a diamant, de Georges Leschot*, illustration from *Les nouvelles conquêtes de la science*, by Louis Figuier, Paris 1883.

**32** The city other

**FIGURE 3.4** Prosper Broux, *Machine Beaumont pour le creusement des tunnels dans les roches tendres*, illustration from *Les nouvelles conquêtes de la science*, by Louis Figuier, Paris 1883.

In this widespread climate of enthusiasm for an underground universe, there have of course been dissenting views, on both theoretical and practical levels. From a philosophical standpoint, architecture built below the ground line, precisely due to its intrinsic nature as architecture without a face, without a facade, without surroundings, is architecture that has lost the transcendent meaning Heidegger outlined so well in the famous example of the bridge.[6] Just as this structure offers no glimpse of the force and intensity it once represented, not embodying the same effort of resistance and the meaning of conjunction of two worlds it had in the past, so underground construction – no longer displaying primeval difficulties of implementation – ends up being perceived as a game in which technique can no longer be recognized, no longer presenting that which lies "behind" the *baukunst*, and rendering the meaning of construction itself banal. Then there is another theoretical order of problems to consider, which links back to the settlements in historical contexts. We are accustomed to seeing a building through what appears on the ground surface:

> je vollständiger ein Denkmal auf uns gekommen ist je authentischer also – desto grösser ist sein Zeugniswert für die Zeit seiner Entstehung. Die Glaubwürdigkeit ist nicht nur abhängig von seiner auf

## The city other  **33**

den ersten Blick sichtbaren Erscheinung, sondern von seiner ganzen materiellen Existenz, nicht nur von den Fassaden also, sondern auch von seinem inneren Aufbau und seiner Umgebung und damit unmittelbar vom Boden, auf dem es steht.[7]

The problems implied by this statement are the irreversibility of projects placed below existing sites, and that of the authenticity of the way a portion of history is transmitted to future generations. The former puts the accent on the impossibility of restoring a prior condition, but also on the lack of possibility to foresee what will happen inside the structure in which the sub-construction will be done: this is true both in the hypothesis of modification of a building, as in the case of an upper addition, and with regard to the impossibility of modifying a structure in reinforced concrete placed below the foundations, if the functions have to subsequently be modified for any reason. If we get away from these practical considerations, the discussion becomes even more complex and problematic, shifting towards the concept of authenticity in architecture. We needn't think about the nevertheless obvious case of archaeological sites or isolated discoveries of relics, for which (almost) always there are national organisms ready to block construction, allowing it to resume only after the operations of digging and cataloguing; we can simply point to the concept of construction as historical evidence, which literally undermines the foundations on which to rest the comprehension of above-ground architecture. Almost a response to the so-called "reverse archaeology" of Zurich, which has applied a very costly strategy, inserting parking facilities, banks, vaults and other functions under the city center.[8] The example indicated by the Swiss Federal Commission on Historic Monuments, referring to the so-called *façadism* of the postwar era – namely the vigorous defense of facades at the expense of internal parts – at first safeguarded the image of streets and entire cities, and then over time has become *Die operettenhafte Kulisse*,[9] an operetta backdrop, of an anachronistic character that becomes immediately obvious when one crosses the boundary, the door, the threshold of houses. Consolidated expedients of disguise of the city, non-choices that beside the cool calculation of the reproduction of warm period facades have permitted concealment of the unwanted content of the building – infrastructural equipment or technical systems unsuitable for viewing – behind existing skeletons of facades (Figure 3.5).[10] Aldo Rossi foresaw this concept, referring to

> those who pretend to preserve the historical cities by retaining their ancient facades or reconstructing them in such a way as to maintain

## 34  The city other

**FIGURE 3.5**  Urban façadism, Rennes 2018 © Antonello Boschi.

their silhouettes and colors and other such things; but what do we find after these operations when they are actually realized? An empty, often repugnant stage.[11]

Curiously enough, in this period of time two diametrically opposed schools of thought have developed, with the pretext of reducing expenditure of land area. There are the advocates of skyscrapers, who assert – or return to the assertion – that tall buildings imply savings in terms of territory: a claim that is certainly far from new, resuscitated first by Koolhaas, calling on the cartoon conceptualizations of Alanson Burton Walker showing a series of traditional houses stacked in a skyscraper structure,[12] underlined by the caption *Buy a cozy cottage in our steel constructed choice lots, less than a mile above Broadway. Only ten minutes by elevator. All the comforts of the country with none of its disadvantages*, then in the utopias of James Wines and SITE with his *Highrise of Homes* (Figure 3.6),[13] and finally in recent years with a coating of environmentalism made of vertical gardens, shrubs clustered on balconies and other green ingredients of the bioclimatic vogue. One example will suffice: the Bosco Verticale (Vertical Forest) in Milan, which according to its designers

**FIGURE 3.6** James Wines, *Highrise of Homes*, 1981 © 2020 James Wines.

helps to set up an urban ecosystem where different kinds of vegetation create a vertical environment which can also be colonized by birds and insects, and thus becomes both a magnet for and a symbol of the spontaneous recolonization of the city by vegetation and by animal life.[14]

In this regard, we can look forward to the enthusiastic applause of the owners in reaction to an invasion of starlings, pigeons, mosquitos and other specimens of biodiversity.

The opposing school of thought insists, in cultural terms, on a sort of telluric spirit,[15] i.e. a return to the land as a reaction against urban density. More concretely, its members – like many people – look at the horrors that crowd our suburbs, the retail outlets, multiplex cinemas or simple production sites, which in the end could easily be hidden from view, one could rightfully assert, in the *camera obscura* of the underground. Even a fierce opponent of this *modus habitandi* like Mumford recognized the fact

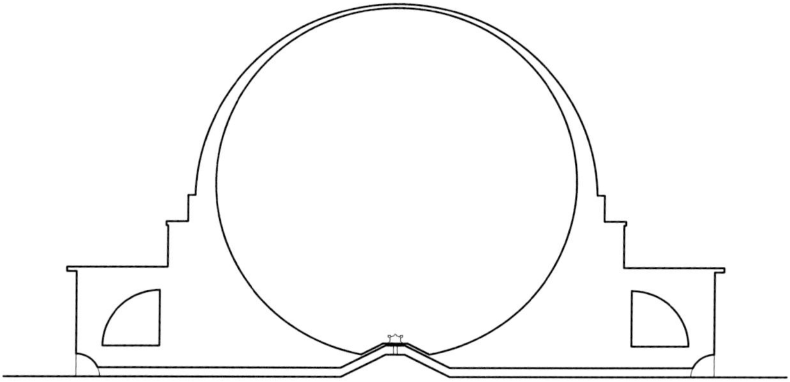

## 36 The city other

**FIGURE 3.7** Section of the Cenotaph for Isaac Newton by Étienne-Louis Boullée, 1784.

that skyscrapers did not permit orientation to the point of raising the issue of whether or not one was over or under the ground. At a distance of centuries, the effect produced in the society of the 1700s by Boullée's Cenotaph for Isaac Newton was repeated (Figure 3.7), or that of the grand hotel by Gaudí for Manhattan with its stacked restaurants never reached by sunlight. This was the effect of a completely above-ground architecture that nevertheless seemed like an underground space[16]; confirmation that it is possible to build upward while making a work of architecture seem underground, and oppositely to create rooms in depth, lighted from above so as to eliminate the anxiety caused by darkness.[17]

Skyscrapers and Landscrapers,[18] *Grattacieli e tunnel* – a set design created by Depero in 1930 to portray the metropolis of New York in a ballet by Leonida Massin, in which buildings and tunnels mingle and interpenetrate – are therefore two sides of the same coin. After all, as Malcolm Wells said, "*Property is 4000 miles deep. Use it*" (Figures 3.8 and 3.9).[19] Though, to be honest, in his manuals the champion of the underground did not envision that house as something buried and eternally in darkness, but as a traditional construction that was then thermally insulated, covered and planted with local species.

The city other 37

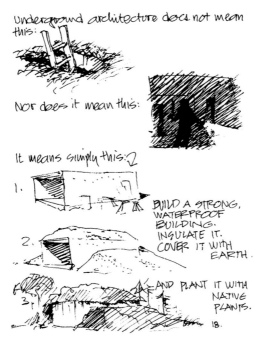

**FIGURE 3.8** Malcolm Wells, *What is underground*, 1995 © Karen North Wells.

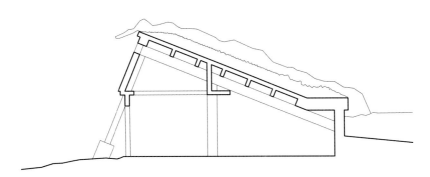

**FIGURE 3.9** Section of the Solaria House by Malcolm Wells, Vinceston 1975.

**38** The city other

**FIGURE 3.10** Section of a rabbit hole © Dorling Kindersley / Alamy Stock Photo.

In both cases, there is a need to shelter in protective architecture, triggering an almost direct parallel between human and animal constructions (Figure 3.10):

> the time is not far off when our planet will cease to provide as much as standing room for its inhabitants. Even if people were able to adapt themselves to a double – or triple – deck civilization, there is a limit to the rank growth of skyscrapers and multilevel highways. The only way out of the human rabbit warren is, quite simply, down the rabbit hole.[20]

Therefore, not just elementary organisms like wasps, ants and insects in general,[21] but also birds and mammals. Hence the rabbit hole desired by Rudofsky and imagined by Lewis Carroll[22] becomes the real Talponia of Gabetti & Isola in Ivrea (Figure 3.11) or the Termite Pavilion at the International Arts Festival of London (Figure 3.12), an installation in which the three-dimensional section of a termite mound was reconstructed on a human scale.

The city other 39

FIGURE 3.11 View of the Western Residential Unit (Talponia) by Roberto Gabetti & Aimaro Isola with Luciano Re, Ivrea 1968–1971 © Antonello Boschi.

FIGURE 3.12 View from below of the Termite Pavilion by Softroom Architects, London 2009 © Joseph Burns.

**40** The city other

The utilitarian functionalism of tombs, sewers, mines and tunnels of the outset has been transformed into the poetic organicism of houses, cultural centers and entertainment facilities of the present, and the *espaces d'hostilité* have been replaced by what Bachelard would call the *espaces d'intimité protégée*.[23] A culture experienced mainly as an expedient, utilized in situations in which the impossibility of traditional construction was evident. The passage from the subterranean of the subconscious to the subterranean of awareness, from cold technology to the city of inhabitable compartments, has certainly not been brief. The beautiful drawings contained in volumes published in the 1960s[24] – nearly always perspective sections or isometric cutaways of subway stations, parking areas or tunnels – narrate an idea of architecture that began by attempting to solve infrastructural problems through the separation of pedestrian and vehicle traffic, and then intertwined relationships and research with sociology and anthropology, though without delving into the territories of construction. Gradually crossing the confines of the individual work, expanding disciplinary perimeters, there has been no lack of comprehensive approaches like those of Chanéac, Erskine, Soleri, Cook, with the various *Villes Cratères*, *Subarctic Cities*, *Novanoah* or *Prepared Landscapes*, whose names already reveal their visionary character.

Prophetically, it was written that

le domaine souterrain est vaste et riche en possibilités. Il est à l'heure actuelle relativement peu exploré. De même qu'un édifice, ne saurait se construire sans ses fondations, la cité de demain ne saurait se passer de l'organisation de son sous-sol. Nous voudrions répandre la notion des villes épaisses car la troisième dimension est nécessaire à l'organisation rationnelle des cités. Une évolution est en cours.[25]

The environmental sensibilities reached in recent decades, the themes of sustainability and consumption of land area, may have transformed the brilliant intuitions of these forerunners into a convincing alternative to cities on the surface of the ground.

Whatever the source of inspiration – troglodytic, animal, environmental – and in spite of the length of the path of approach, the sensation remains of having finally freed the underground from the burdensome cultural legacy that has permeated its image across the centuries, of being able to finally discuss the "below" without anxieties, an ablative architecture to observe without preconceived judgments, of a city that does not vanish, but finds new collocations.

# Notes

1 Cinzia Bearzot, "La città che scompare. Corinto, Tespie e Platea tra autonomia cittadina e politeiai alternative," in *In limine. Ricerche su marginalità e periferia nel mondo antico*, eds. Gabriella Vanotti, and Claudia Perassi (Milan: V&P università, 2004), 269–284.

2 "… the unique and final city raises its stainless walls, I am collecting the ashes of the other possible cities that vanish to make room for it, cities that can never be rebuilt or remembered." In Italo Calvino, *Invisible Cities* (New York: Harcourt Brace Jovanovich, 1974), 60.

3 Ibid., 142, 16.

4 Antonello Boschi, "La piccola città invisibile," *Rassegna* 87 (June 2007): 80–89.

5 In 1933 Utudjian founded G.E.C.U.S. (*Groupe d'Études et de Coordination de l'Urbanisme Souterrain) that tried to make the general public aware of housing possibilities of la ville épaisseur.*

6 Martin Heidegger, *Building Dwelling Thinking* (New York: Harper Colophon Books, 1971).

7 Bernhard Furrer, "Unterirdische Bauten im historischen Bereich – ein Grundsatzpapier der Eidgenössischen Kommission für Denkmalpflege," *Nike Bulletin* 4 (December 2001): 11. "The more intact a monument has come to us – and thus the more authentic – the greater its testimony regarding the time of its creation. Its credibility depends not only on its appearance at first glance, but also its entire material existence, not only on the facades but also its internal structure and surroundings, and thus directly on the ground on which it stands."

8 Rem Koolhaas, "The Generic City," in O.M.A., Rem Koolhaas, and Bruce Mau, *S, M, L, XL: Small, Medium, Large, Extra-Large*, ed. Jennifer Sigler (New York: The Monacelli Press, 1995), 1249.

9 Furrer, "Unterirdische Bauten im historischen Bereich," 15.

10 Rafael Gómez-Moriana, "Il mascheramento quotidiano nella città. Il paradosso dell'occultamento per assimilazione con il contesto urbano," *Lotus* 126 (November 2005): 126–137.

11 Aldo Rossi, *The Architecture of the City* (Cambridge, MA: MIT Press, 1982), 123.

12 Alanson Burton Walker, "Cartoon," *Life* 1375 (March 4, 1909): 299. Then in Rem Koolhaas, *Delirious New York: A Retroactive Manifesto for Manhattan* (New York: The Monacelli Press, 1994), 83.

13 Patricia Philips, and James Wines, *The Highrise of Homes / Site* (New York: Rizzoli, 1982), 41.

14 Stefano Boeri, "Bosco Verticale," *Area* 122 (May–June 2012): 102.

15 Paul Virilio, in François Burkhardt, and Paul Virilio, "Abbiamo bisogno del sottosuolo," *Domus* 879 (March 2005), 110. Virilio's passion for a "solid" architecture can be seen in many of his writings when he criticizes the "craze for transparency at any cost, the art of an architecture of light in which iron and glass take over from brick and stone, along with concrete, now so on the nose. This process has even gone as far, most recently, as using techniques for suspending glass cladding that are directly inspired by aeronautical construction, to reinforce, further and further, the impression of lightness, of weightlessness, of a massive building wildy trying to be not so much real as virtual." In Paul Virilio, *Art as far as the eye can see* (Oxford: Berg, 2007), 50–51.

**42** The city other

16 See Emanuele Fidone, "La dimensione ipogeica dell'architettura fra Settecento e Ottocento," in *The Time of Schinkel and the Age of Neoclassicism between Palermo and Berlin*, eds. Maria Giuffrè, Paola Barbera, and Gabriella Cianciolo Cosentino (Cannitello, RC: Biblioteca del Cenide, 2006), 159–172.

17 Hans Hollein, "Tutto è architettura, François Burkhardt intervista Hans Hollein," *Rassegna* 87 (2007): 22–29.

18 Betsky, *Landscrapers: Building with the Land*. The neologism *Landscrapers* was actually coined by Antoine Predock.

19 Cf. among the many volumes of the author, Malcolm Wells, *Gentle Architecture* (New York: McGraw-Hill, 1981); Malcolm Wells, *Underground Designs* (Andover, MA: Brick House, 1977).

20 Rudofsky, *The Prodigious Builders*, 44–45.

21 See Karl von Frisch, *Animal Architecture* (New York: Harcourt Brace Jovanovich, 1974).

22 Lewis Carroll, *Alice's Adventures in Wonderland* (Boston, MA: Lee and Shepard, 1869), 1–14.

23 Bachelard, *The Poetics of Space*, xxxvi, 3.

24 See for all Édouard Utudjian, *Architecture et Urbanisme souterrains* (Paris: Robert Laffont, 1966).

25 Édouard Utudjian, *L'urbanisme souterrain* (Paris: Presses Universitaires de France, 1964), 126.

> The underground domain is vast and rich in possibilities. It is currently relatively unexplored. Just as a building cannot be constructed without its foundations, the city of tomorrow cannot be built without its foundations, without the organization of its part below. We would like to spread the notion of *thick* cities, because the third dimension is necessary for their rational organization. An evolution is in progress.

# 4
# MIMICRY

We have seen how Utudjian, with his *ville épaisse*, foreshadowed the concept of territory as a limited resource. His proposal of three-dimensional zoning, while not solving the problems of the modern city, took an opposing stance to the *ville en étendue* and the *ville en hauteur*,[1] while its rejection of the assumption of Le Corbusier and the skyscrapers of New York placed it at the opposite extreme of the reigning theories on detachment from the ground.

In particular, there is a not-very-technical but very effective drawing, in symbolic terms, which in the Swiss Pavilion in Paris (Figure 4.1) reveals all the inconsistencies of one of the Five Points of Architecture with respect to the choice of the place of construction. To safeguard the building's typology, the Swiss architect was forced to sink the pilotis of the foundation into the bowels of the earth, due to the presence not of natural caverns, but of an old filled-in quarry. A model – that of the "reinforced concrete [with which] you get rid of walls completely. [...] To found them, a small well is dug out for each one down to good soil. Then the column is raised above ground"[2] – that displayed its lack of foundation, its abstract nature, with definitive drawings that revealed only the emerging portion, *radieuse*, of an unintentional subterranean construction.[3] Its theoretical contribution is well known: the comparison between the area occupied by the *traditional stone house* and that utilized for a *house in reinforced concrete or iron* revealed a difference of 140% in favor of the raised house and roof garden, and of as much as 180% regarding free circulation of automobiles and pedestrians.[4]

DOI: 10.4324/9781003214960-4

## 44 Mimicry

**FIGURE 4.1** Section of the Swiss Pavilion in the Cité Universitaire of Le Corbusier, 1930 © FLC.

What Le Corbusier did not foresee is that in place of a new civilization of habitation capable of altering the appearance and functioning of the metropolis, cities themselves would gradually spread into the countryside, accomplishing the brilliant *calembour* of Commerson: *il faudrait construire les villes à la campagne, l'air y est plus sain*.[5] The reports prepared by the European Environmental Agency demonstrate the exponential growth of urbanized areas with respect to agricultural areas in recent decades, and show that Italy has established itself as the frontrunner in these transformations. It is not just a problem of consumption of resources, greenhouse gas emissions or climate change; it is not, in a word whose efficacy has been depleted, at this point, just a matter of sustainability: it is a cultural problem. The alteration of the earth's surface by humankind has always existed and has grown, keeping pace with the unstoppable growth of the population. What has changed is where and how these changes manifest themselves. The traditional city-country dichotomy has weakened under the pressure of that mixture of types known as "urban sprawl,"[6] a sort of no-man's-land, a "gray zone" as Levi put it made of disheartening suburbs that do not belong in either of the two original categories. The abandonment of the *forma urbis* has produced the so-called *"espaces indécis,"*[7] the scattering of habitation, the saturation of every available area and at the same time a construction *in extenso* that leaves many indistinct, amorphous, leftover gaps. "There is something enervating about a landscape neither predominantly free of building nor tightly compacted, but littered with towers distributed without respect for edges or lines, a landscape which denies us the true pleasures of both nature and urbanisation."[8] The first warnings of this phenomenon were noted at the start of the 1900s with the growth of industry, the increase of the population, the extension of average life expectancy due to the conquests of medicine, and the spread of literacy to millions of people. The problem of the SLOAP[9] then became more acute after World War II, fed by the increasing rejection of urban density and the modernization of the society,[10] to the point of giving rise to a condition of urban sprawl (Figure 4.2). What had once been the allure of Italy – though it was not yet a nation, but a sum of principalities and republics – prompted writers, painters and travelers to set off on the *grand*

**FIGURE 4.2** Suburban living in the postwar era, Levittown 1958 © Joseph Scherschel / The LIFE Picture Collection via Getty Images.

**46** Mimicry

*Tour* and to focus their interest on a *Voyage en Italie*. In spite of geographical, social and cultural differences,

> until the end of the 1800s, (almost) no one who built something (almost) ever erred, and a single idea of dignity and appropriateness was embodied in the house and the palace, the cathedral and the chapel deep in the woods.[11]

Differences of purpose and location notwithstanding, all the settlement principles had an air of familiarity, as the expression of a local culture, a shared way of doing things, a common sentiment. It should be emphasized that we are not talking about a crystallized, immobile, inert scenario, but simply a landscape that was not subjected to transformations but accompanied by them, a time that was not schizophrenic but slow and well-pondered.

The exploitation of areas of environmental value has led to the need to reformulate habitual design approaches. While the ongoing urban growth of the diffused city, its infrastructures and its networks generate more and more compromised areas, the question arises as to which strategies can be applied to transform, widen and change the conventional relationship between abuse of land and lack of use of the ground underneath it. The examples of inept or damaging use of land, the destruction of the "views" to which we were accustomed, may vary from the "epidemic" of prefabrication in the countryside of the Veneto,[12] to the Ager Romanus "plowed" by the real estate speculators, to a Campania that is certainly no longer *Das Land Wo die Zitronen blühen*,[13] or the millions of cubic meters of concrete that for twenty years, from 1955 to 1975, took the place of a portion of the Palermo panorama immortalized by 19th-century veduta painters, filmed by Visconti in the cinematic version of *The Leopard*, or narrated in words by Guy de Maupassant:

> The city is surrounded by that forest of orange trees which has been called 'the shell of gold,' and this forest of black verdure spreads like a dark stain at the foot of grayish and reddish mountains [...] A continuous breeze that enraptures the mind and disturbs the senses. [...] This odor surrounds one, mingling the refined sensation of perfumes with the artistic joys of the mind, throws you for a few seconds into a well-being of mind and body that is almost happiness.[14]

Starting from a geographical context often cited as an example, such as that of "*Toscana Felix*," marked by the artful naturalism of a certain type

Mimicry **47**

of countryside, where from the coast to the inland hills the territories are pervaded by environmental and manmade excellence, the accent falls on the dichotomy between widespread needs of growth and respect for the ecosystem, on the utopia-reality dualism of an underground architecture that instead of prompting disquiet can and should be seen as a resource. Works of architecture below ground level that can respond to the need for great volumes in shopping centers, multiplex cinemas, or activities of crafts and production inserted in systems of construction and circulation. Indicative cases exist of projects that have not moved in the direction of recovery of existing structures, nor towards experimentation with models of new construction capable of protecting and enhancing various specific contexts. We are thinking about the controversial episode of the "terraced villas" of Monticchiello in the municipality of Pienza, a contradiction in typological terms and a travesty in ecological terms[15]; about the practice of placing windmills not only in dramatically hilly locations but also in (at this point) damaged plains – seen, correctly or not, as "everyone's back yard"[16] – where the only vestige of ecology lives on in the term "park" used to indicate a mere cluster of wind turbines (Figure 4.3); about the open scars torn open by quarries, which of course also existed in the past, but now give rise to vaguely lunar landscapes. Not to mention the aerial power lines with their pylons painted green, in a pathetic attempt at camouflage in the landscape. We might conclude that the only panorama left

**FIGURE 4.3** The visual impact of a wind park on a hill © Antonello Boschi.

## 48 Mimicry

intact is the one described by poets, novelists and intellectuals, or depicted by Italian and foreign artists; nothing real, in short, nothing like the view from a window, but only what has been captured in the pages of a book or inside the frame of a painting.

A concrete example of this progressive process of decline is the construction of a major road leading from Fano to Grosseto. This was the so-called *Due Mari*, which like many works of this size was implemented – and at times even designed – "along the way." If we consider the famous diptych of the Dukes of Urbino by Piero della Francesca (Figure 4.4), and especially the background of the portraits of Battista Sforza and Federico da Montefeltro and their Triumphs, for many years it was thought that the horizons, evoking the example of Flemish painting, were totally imaginary. Research recently conducted, however, demonstrates that those hills, that lake and those forests actually existed, and coincide with the Metauro Valley straddling the towns of Urbania, Fermignano, Urbino and Acqualagna.[17] Unfortunately for these scenes, which many believe were immortalized in the so-called balconies of Piero della Francesca, the E78 highway had an equally great period of implementation, almost fifty years,

**FIGURE 4.4** The hidden landscape in *The diptych of the Dukes of Urbino* by Piero della Francesca, 1465–1472 © su concessione del Ministero per i Beni e le Attività Culturali e per il Turismo – Gallerie degli Uffizi.

launched by Amintore Fanfani at the end of the 1960s. The portion that concerns us was to pass along the margins of the valley with a route mostly in tunnels, while a variation proposed by an Austrian firm called for a road that would practically cut the valley in two.

A typically Italian setting, already rich in its own right with complex morphological situations, which truly owes much to the geological *longue durée*, the centuries-long rhythms of nature, but also the fast rhythms of the action of man, the two shaping actions of excavation and infill.[18] "Since the fate of man is to live by the sweat of his brow, any civilized country is distinguished from a wild one in that it is an immense hard work store. It was by hard work that the houses, river banks, and canals were built. Perhaps three thousand years have passed since the people bent their backs over this primitive moorland and removed the last residue of the native harshness from it."[19] Excavation was done for economic motives – extraction of materials for construction and cladding – and due to necessity – making foundations, but also tunnels, wells, passages, embankments. Excavation was done to seek the vestiges of the past in a landscape that can be seen as a repository of traces, where its study is like a stratified history of places. But after having given form to utopias, and at times having excavated for no reason at all, the time has come to repair the fragile signs that have been passed down to us by generations. While it would be unthinkable to completely erase infrastructure works of great impact like railroads and highways, where the "bellowing fire" of Ruskin and the "roaring motorcar" of Marinetti have contributed to a globalized geography, much can be done on an architectural plane. The typical alienation and detachment with respect to what exists, made of *terrains artificiels* capable of resolving inextricable topographies,[20] can be countered by strategies of *mimesis* – which have well-known historical-artistic forerunners[21] – tactics of concealment, relying on the immateriality of architecture, on transparency, glass, but also on the reflection of the surrounding space. An "ecological" ploy that always poses the problem of a reflecting form, long considered a valid system of camouflage which certainly adapts better to nature, as in the Mimetic House in the Irish countryside (Figure 4.5)[22] or in urban contexts like the pioneering Willis Faber & Dumas Headquarters building in Ipswich or the recent *Glass Farm* at Schijndel (Figure 4.6).

There exists a third way, however, to make the visible invisible (Figure 4.7),[23] which is that of simply burying the architecture. An apparently banal method, but one that permits the *natura naturata* of a work to blend with the *natura naturans* of the zone. And precisely the Tuscan countryside – marked by a design of the land as an organization of requirements, where

50 Mimicry

FIGURE 4.5 View of the Mimetic House by Dominic Stevens, Dromaheir 2007 © Ros Kavanagh.

FIGURE 4.6 The reflecting effect of the glass on the surrounding construction in the Glass Farm by MVRDV, Schijndel 2013 © MVRDV.

Mimicry 51

**FIGURE 4.7** Example of camouflage during World War II over the Lochkeed factory in Burbank, 1942 © Lockheed Martin.

geography and history take on a stable configuration through the furrows, bends, coverings, raised parts, borders, mergers and repairs typical of rural culture – offers us the premises to compare two typologically similar projects. Let's take one of the first instances of collaboration between an architect and a major wine producer: we are at the end of the 1990s, and on the hill of Suvereto, inland from Piombino, Mario Botta opts for a partial burial of the winery to cope with the production process (Figure 4.8) – from the pressing of the grapes to the final shipping of the wine – and the reinterpretation of the country villa through a cylindrical body dissected by an inclined plane and two volumes with porticos at the sides. The perception[24] in this plain in Maremma is that of an object morphologically out of place – and in fact it has shade thanks to the typical "*barchesse*" of Venetian villas (Figure 4.9) – and also out of scale, with the air of an *object trouvé*: little has been remedied over the years with the growth of the olive trees placed at the top of the building to attenuate its impact. The forceful gesture gets the better of the context, perhaps for the worse. By contrast,

## 52  Mimicry

**FIGURE 4.8**  Section through Cantina Petra by Mario Botta, Suvereto 2003.

**FIGURE 4.9**  View of Cantina Petra by Mario Botta, Suvereto 2003 © Antonello Boschi.

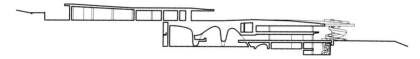

**FIGURE 4.10**  Section through Cantina Antinori by Archea Associati, Bargino 2012.

the winery by Archea at Bargino (Figure 4.10)[25] – on one of the many slopes of Chianti – conveys the memory of the underground, the echoes of a product that is born from and develops from the ground, in a deep bond with the *terroir*, to the point of being hidden inside it, mingling with it. A completely buried enclosure, without walls, roads or parking areas, with the facade spreading on the natural slope shaped by rows of vines, which

Mimicry 53

FIGURE 4.11  View of Cantina Antinori by Archea Associati, Bargino 2012, ©
Pietro Savorelli courtesy Archea.

FIGURE 4.12  Caravaggio, *The Incredulity of Saint Thomas*, 1600–1601 © su concessione del Ministero per i beni e le attività culturali e per il Turismo – Gallerie degli Uffizi.

**54** Mimicry

with the soil are its sole covering (Figure 4.11). Adapting to the curves of shifting levels, subtle openings reveal – without emphasis – the inner core of the winery, and for once the wounds inflicted on the landscape are literal, incisions, lacerations, cuts that can be completely mended. Not a minor, hidden, defeatist work of architecture, not an architecture "in the negative," where the expression itself already conveys a relative judgment, but – to paraphrase Merleau-Ponty[26] – an architecture so steeped in non-being as to appear as only what it is. "At bottom," *la noirceur secrète du lait* [...] *n'est accessible qu'à travers sa blancheur* (Figure 4.12).

## Notes

1 Utudjian, *L'urbanisme souterrain*, 29.
2 Le Corbusier, "Techniques Are the Very Basis of Poetry," in *Precisions on the Present State of Architecture and City Planning: with an American prologue, a Brazilian corollary followed by The temperature of Paris and The atmosphere of Moscow* (Cambridge, MA: MIT Press, 1991), 38. The abandonment of the foundations instead of the pilotis is a theme that Le Corbusier treats since his first writings. See Le Corbusier, *Towards a New Architecture* (Mineola, NY: Dover, 1986), 60.
3 See Francesco Venezia, "Incidenti a reazione poetica," *Domus* 681 (March 1987): 46.
4 Le Corbusier, "Techniques Are the Very Basis of Poetry," 41.
5 Jean-Louis-Auguste Commerson, *Pensées d'un emballeur: pour faire suite aux Maximes de La Rochefoucauld* (Paris: Martinon, 1851), 124: "Cities should be built in the country, the air is healthier."
6 See Richard Ingersoll, *Sprawltown. Looking for the City on Its Edges* (New York: Princeton Architectural Press, 2006); Maria Cristina Gibelli, and Edoardo Salzano, eds., *No Sprawl: perché è necessario controllare la dispersione urbana e il consumo di suolo* (Firenze: Alinea, 2006).
7 Gilles Clément, *Manifeste du Tiers paysage* (Paris: Sujet-objet éd., 2004), 12.
8 Alain de Botton, *The Architecture of Happiness* (London: Penguin, 2007), 245.
9 There is another term to indicate this phenomenon, SLOAP, Space Left Over After Planning, that is what remains vague, unresolved, indefinite after the project, coined for the first time during the energy crisis of the 1970s. See Leslie B. Ginsburg, "Summing up," *The Architectural Review* 920 (October 1973): 264.
10 See the shift of Abu Simbel due to the construction of the Aswan dam, as an example of the artificial construction of the postwar nature desire. In Michael Jakob, *Le paysage* (Gollion: Infolio editions, 2008), 11.
11 Salvatore Settis, *Paesaggio Costituzione Cemento. La battaglia per l'ambiente contro il degrado civile* (Turin: Einaudi, 2010), 53.
12 See Tiziano Tempesta, "L'uso del suolo nei pressi delle ville venete: un'indagine su scala regionale," in *Alla ricerca del paesaggio palladiano. Un'indagine sul paesaggio delle ville venete in età contemporanea* (Legnaro: University of Padova, 2015), 133–162.
13 Johann Wolfgang Goethe, *Wilhelm Meister's Years of Apprenticeship* (Richmond, Surrey: Alma Classics, 2013), 107. "The land where lemons are in flower."

Mimicry **55**

14 Guy de Maupassant, "Sicily," in *La Vie Errante and Others Stories* (New York: J.H. Sears & Company Inc., 1922), 55–56.

15 In that period, Asor Rosa spoke of mockery and "eco-monsters."

16 The reference is to the well-known acronym NIMBY, Not In My Back Yard.

17 Rosetta Borchia, and Olivia Nesci, *The Invisible Landscape: Discovering the Real Landscapes of Piero della Francesca* (Ancona: Il lavoro editoriale, 2012).

18 Ludovico Micara, s.v. "Scavare/Colmare," in *Manuale. Forme insediative e infrastrutture*, ed. Aimaro Oreglia d'Isola (Venice: Marsilio, 2002), 306–308.

19 Carlo Cattaneo, "Industria e Morale," in *Alcuni scritti*, vol. 3 (Milan: Bonomi e Scotti, 1846): 267.

20 Think of the plans for Algiers, Montevideo, Rio de Janeiro by Le Corbusier so artificial and indifferent in the modeling of the ground with respect to the conformation of places.

21 For art see the relationship between cubism and camouflage in Gertrude Stein, *The autobiography of Alice B. Toklas* (New York: The Literary Guild, 1933) and Gertrude Stein, *Picasso* (London: B. T. Batsford, 1938). For the evolution in the camouflage of military vehicles of the World War I become, through various techniques, tool of camouflage of ships, factories, parts of the inhabited area see Roy R. Behrens, "Architecture, Art and Camouflage. L'origine militare del camouflage ad opera di un gruppo di artisti dell'esercito americano," *Lotus* 126 (November 2005): 75–83.

22 Antonello Boschi, "Architettura en travesti: mimetismi, camuffamenti e altri espedienti urbani," 43. On these topics see Neil Leach, *Camouflage* (Cambridge, MA: MIT Press, 2006) and Chiara Casarin, and Davide Fornari, eds., *Estetiche del camouflage* (Milan: et al., 2010).

23 See Eugenio Turri, "Il visibile e l'invisibile del paesaggio," in *Il paesaggio e il silenzio* (Venice: Marsilio, 2004), 67–84.

24 For the difference between territory and landscape see Carlo Tosco, *Il paesaggio come storia* (Bologna: Il Mulino, 2007), 118:

> the landscape is distinguished from the territory because it includes the dimension of perception and form of the manmade environment. […] Passing from the territory to the landscape, we do not pass from its material structure to the field of abstract ideas and aesthetics, but from the material structure to the cultural perception of space.

25 Boschi, "La piccola città invisibile," 88.

26 Maurice Merleau-Ponty, *The Visible and the Invisible: Followed by Working Notes*, ed. Claude Laffort (Evanston, IL: Northwestern University Press, 1968), 150. "As the secret blackness of milk, […] is accessible only through its whiteness." Actually the author attributes the phrase to Paul Valery.

# 5
## NOVELTY IS BUT OBLIVION

If there is a place that combines the past, present and future of a housing typology, it is Matmata (Figure 5.1), a Berber village on the arid plains of southern Tunisia. Here a population of a few hundred souls continues to live in caves dug into the perimeter walls of enormous craters with a diameter of about twenty meters, and a depth of six to twelve meters, depending on the number of residential levels. Access to the individual homes is provided by these natural courtyards, like neighborhood squares capable of containing up to a hundred inhabitants, true community spaces connected to the land surface by means of sloping tunnels, whose sides have been hollowed out to make toolsheds, storerooms for victuals and shelters for animals.[1] The patios are at times adorned by plants like palms and eucalyptus, with a central cistern for rainwater. They are reached by way of a long inclined ramp wide enough for the passage of camels. The rooms are from four to seven meters in length, three to four in width, by a height of about three meters. Everything has been dug into the rock, from the place to spread a carpet for sleeping to the cavities cut into the walls to contain objects. Leading to the rooms on the upper level, the steps are carved into the terrain or made with pieces of wood inserted in the structure, starting from the bottom of the pit (Figure 5.2).[2]

These are dwellings that are not just shelters from the extreme heat and sandstorms, but also – with their presence, or more precisely their absence – give rise to *invisible cities* capable of standing up to attacks by nomadic bands. Houses that began as individual spaces but then spread like weeds on

DOI: 10.4324/9781003214960-5

Novelty is but oblivion 57

FIGURE 5.1  View from above of cave dwellings, Matmata © Reuters/Zohra Bensemra.

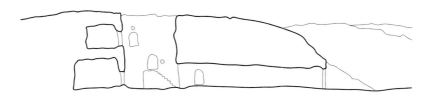

FIGURE 5.2  Plan and section of a house on two levels, Matmata.

## 58 Novelty is but oblivion

unploughed land, connecting larger rooms to minimum spaces by means of corridors, passages and doors. Dwellings that with their wall niches and vaulted ceilings have developed into a complex system of labyrinthine spaces that create true underground weaves.

It was no coincidence that George Lucas, director, and John Barry, set designer, chose these constructions as the elective abode of Luke Skywalker in the initial episode of the *Star Wars* saga (Figure 5.3). A timeless house that had remained unchanged across the centuries, which with a few artful touches such as the presence of vaporizers or a metal door with a strange opening device could be projected into another galaxy and another temporal dimension. The recognition factor of this place is such that it has been permanently inserted in the tour of sets for film lovers, though with some unexpected effects for the local population: the tourists clustered around these craters seem to observe the everyday activities of their inhabitants with the same astonishment prompted in the past by the sight of bears in certain zoos.

**FIGURE 5.3** The courtyard of Luke Skywalker's house, in a still taken from *Star Wars*, by George Lucas, USA 1977: with set design featuring vaporizers and a metal door.

We are used to thinking about housing typologies along the crystallized lines of the isolated house, the tower, row housing, condominium, balcony-access buildings. Of course there have been attempts to shuffle the deck, trying to reproduce from scratch the mixture of functions typical of the historical city in mixed and hybrid buildings. Yet there exists a way of living that does not require vertical or horizontal development, but retreats into itself: a way of living below the surface of the earth, literally sinking into the terrain. This is certainly not a new type, but the use made of underground spaces across history has always had a provisional tone, limited to short time spans, and generally without residential purposes. It was thought that working underground could be an acceptable compromise, a few hours below the surface after which to emerge and rebehold the stars, and that in the end claustrophobia, fear, anxiety and certain "psychosomatic" ailments could be controlled with minor adjustments to optical, climatic and design factors. Actually an enormous quantity of studies, especially from countries where underground work was the norm, such as China, demonstrated that the problems were terribly real.[3] These studies have turned out to be useful in order to understand the path to be taken in the passage from the transhumance of labor to situations of settlement. In theoretical terms, a good starting point to understand what kind of underground house can best adapt to the needs of contemporary man might be that of a ranking, indicating advantages and disadvantages, virtues and drawbacks, particularities and weak points for each typology. Not that such rankings do not exist; there may even be too many, since they pivot on extremely heterogeneous criteria. But the problem is not to make a catalogue, but to find some agreement on its terms. We can think of a lexicon that sets out to define the various types on the basis of their materials, such as stone (petratectural), sand (psammotectural), clay (argillatectural) or earth (terratectural),[4] or the more subtle divisions of construction into geotecture, lithotecture, terratecture.[5]

Among the many, some have a general character,[6] others are more specific, based on the topography *of* the terrain, the position *in* the terrain or the use of spaces in time, i.e. if they are occupied on a seasonal or settled basis.[7] Or they can be divided in terms of the form they create, namely if they are raised above the earth line creating an embankment – the berm type – or recessed into the ground – the subgrade type.[8] Furthermore, increasing in complexity, there can be a taxonomy almost on a botanical basis, with division, class, subclass, order, type, subtype and species, as formulated by Baggs at the start of the 1980s,[9] or the more comprehensive version of Sterling.[10]

## 60 Novelty is but oblivion

What seems to be missing in the narration of the underground dwelling is the symmetry with comparable above-ground typological analysis, focusing on horizontal or vertical development, spaces of circulation, modes of aggregation. In this sense we can identify three macro-typologies: the cliff house, the earth-sheltered house and the pit house.

The first can be seen as the "natural" evolution of troglodyte architecture, a cave dug into the slope of a hill with a single entrance offering a view of the panorama. While in the past digging deeper was an advantage for the conservation of food provisions or the storage of materials, over time the widening of the open front took over from horizontal penetration, bringing more direct sunlight to the interiors. The evolution of this type gave rise to two approaches to the spatial layout. When the living spaces shift towards the light, corridors and atria move into the depths of the hill, while when the circulation spaces are in the light it becomes necessary to make another cut in the ridge to illuminate the rooms below by means of light wells, solar chimneys or courts. Thus the vertical section is inevitably simple, with the sole variations provided by the different heights or depths of the rooms or the various construction systems such as flat ceilings, vaults or curved sections.

The earth-sheltered house (Figure 5.4) is the type that has had the most success in the 20th century, especially in the United States, precisely due to the different theoretical formulation on which it "stands." A house that finds fertile ground in terms of camouflage, apparent respect for nature and recycling of primary energy sources, in the 1970s and 1980s when a major energy crisis posed a challenge to the classic ways of building and living. In this perspective, we can consider the paradigmatic contribution on levels of both implementation and exegesis of Malcolm Wells.[11] His focus was actually on a dwelling constructed partially or totally above ground and subsequently covered with earth. Precisely due to this additive and not subtractive approach, perhaps it cannot even be considered an underground structure, and in fact that limitations from a design standpoint are non-existent regarding the height of the spaces, the proportions, exposure,

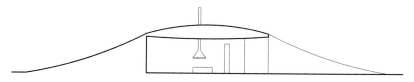

**FIGURE 5.4** Earth-sheltered house, section of the Malator House by Future Systems, Milford Haven, 1994–1996.

geology of the terrain and drainage of water. The earthy covering brings the benefits of underground living to a work of architecture that does not belong to that category.

The pit house (Figure 5.5) is the type whose excavated spaces without visual contact with the context make it the epitome of all the fears of "burial," a negative sculpture, a pit in which the space itself is the form of the architecture.[12] Though it is an inward-probing organism, its position in level terrain does not influence the quantity of light that reaches its rooms: it will suffice to proportion the height of the windows with respect to the breadth of the pit, and portions of sizeable horizontal depth of the building can be reached. The key element is therefore the trench and the rooms that are placed around it, giving rise to a sort of patio, a court with a more or less circular or quadrangular form. While in the cliff house the horizontal expansion is limited by the sunlight, the multilevel organization of the pit house is instead much more manageable, since it is connected to the breadth of the opening that captures the light. Here we see a layout scheme in which the living area is inserted in contact with the glass fronts on the courtyard, while the bedroom zones are arranged on the upper levels or protected by porticos. Drawing the section, we can clearly see the stacking of the internal spaces, which wind up facing each other.

The virtue of having a single outlet towards the outside, towards the sky, is also this house's limitation. This problem was already addressed by Trinquesse, imagining a utopian civilization in the now imminent year of 2025, living in underground abodes equipped with a tropical garden and a pool of water, almost a bioclimatic sphere that in the author's intentions would act a reminder of the nature existing several meters away, up on the earth's surface.[13] A courtyard that would no longer be limited to a mere hole from which to gain daylight, but would permit us to get our temporal and spatial bearings, preventing the labyrinth effect,[14] in a lowering of the natural context that would simultaneously provide shade and privacy for the inhabitants. A patio as "heaven's watercourse," as Borges would have said.[15]

**FIGURE 5.5** Pit house, section of the Earth House by BCHO Architects, Jipyeong-myeon, 2008–2009.

**62** Novelty is but oblivion

Having identified the pit and cliff houses (Figure 5.6), as the two main macro-typologies, it is important to emphasize another aspect that can determine the composition of the spaces, namely the itinerant use or nomadism of internal settings. It is possible, in fact, to utilize areas without assigning them precise, stable functions, instead opting to sleep, cook and spend time in different rooms during different periods of the year. For example, in the summer and in hot-arid climates the most common functional requirements during the day, those of living areas, studies and kitchens, could be carried out in the places with least sunlight, while the nighttime zone could be located in the area with the greatest solar radiation across the day, possibly screened off and/or darkened to avoid absorbing heat and then releasing it during the night.[16] Likewise, during the winter the living areas could be moved closer to the sunlight, in contact with the windows, while seeking maximum thermal protection for sleeping in the other parts of the house at the back.[17] While it is clear that the nomadism of parts like the cooking facilities would be hard to accomplish without duplication, it would be possible to intervene with a more limited seasonal nomadism, using different parts of the dwelling in different periods of the year, or a daily nomadism, inhabiting various levels and spaces at different times of day.[18]

While up to this point we have focused on single dwellings, it becomes indispensable to shift to a larger scale and to examine the passage from the individual house to groupings of houses. Manuals on above-ground housing are filled with tables that help us to understand the mechanisms of its composition, aggregation and association. Some attempt to analyze their evolution, while others simply indicate the possibilities of combination.

Less freedom is permitted in the grouping of underground housing. Just as we have eliminated the earth-sheltered house as a disguised type, so we now have to eliminate the settlement potential of the cliff house. It is true

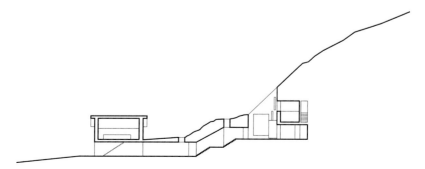

**FIGURE 5.6** Cliff house, section of a private villa by SeARCH + CMA, Vals, 2005–2009.

## Novelty is but oblivion   63

that on a crest each single residence, by directly facing a path cut into the rock, can give rise through horizontal juxtaposition to a sort of balcony that permits independent entry to the houses, which share perimeter walls as in the case of row housing. It is also true that this clustering can happen vertically, in the section, by the stacking of modules connected by external paths, constructing an overall infrastructural system. Nevertheless, the environmental impact of this type of arrangement is and remains very strong.

We can only turn our attention to the past, to villages in Tunisia but also Turkey, India, China (Figures 5.7 and 5.8). Places in which the characteristic pit formation permits grouping around a single open space that transforms the private character of the courtyard into a context of social gathering. Here, in the case of residence on a single level, access can be provided by a single staircase that connects a system of external balconies, or through multiple staircases leading to the various housing units.

The number and size of the individual modules are obviously proportionate to the size of the court, in terms of area and depth of the excavation, creating repeatable but always independent units and, through addition, an urban grid. This modular approach has been applied, though not for residential use, in the UNESCO offices in Paris, and it reminds us of a version – like a negative, lowered into the ground – of the Plan Cerdá in Barcelona

**FIGURE 5.7**   View from above of the houses in Sanmenxia, Henan Province, China.

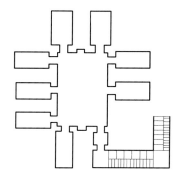

**FIGURE 5.8** Plan and section of a house with a sunken courtyard, Sanmenxia.

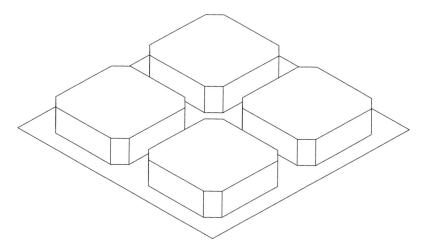

**FIGURE 5.9** Three-dimensional plan of the blocks of Ildefons Cerdà's plan, Barcelona, 1859.

(Figure 5.9), where an entire portion of the city was designed based on a checkerboard layout that placed a block with an internal courtyard on each of the lots.

A return to vertical development seen from a different perspective, namely from below (Figure 5.10). No longer the building that replaces the

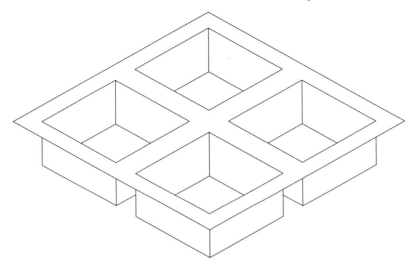

FIGURE 5.10  Three-dimensional plan of a possible underground city with inner courtyards.

earth, the original sin of architecture,[19] but only free, open horizons. Accustomed to traditional housing typologies, we discover – as John Donne put it – that "all novelty is but oblivion."

## Notes

1  Kenneth B. Labs, "The Architectural Underground," *Underground Space* 1 (May–June, 1976): 2. See David Kempe, *Living Underground. A History of Cave and Cliff Dwelling* (London: The Herbert Press, 1988), 136–137.
2  Jean-Paul Loubes, *Archi troglo* (Roquevaire: Parenthèses, 1984), 60.
3  See Antonello Boschi, "Sotterranei dell'anima," in Antonello Boschi, and Giorgio Croatto, *Filosofia del nascosto. Costruire, pensare, abitare nel sottosuolo* (Venice: Marsilio, 2015), 21–28.
4  Gideon S. Golany, *Earth-Sheltered Habitat: History, Architecture and Urban Design* (New York: Van Nostrand Reinhold, 1983), 4.
5  Collected for the first time by Labs in his Master's thesis in 1975, some definitions had been previously coined by Royce LaNier, *Geotecture* (Paris: University of Notre Dame, 1970), Patrick Horsbrugh, "Urban Geotecture: The Invisible Features of the Civic Profile," in *Proceedings of the Conference on Alternatives in Energy Conservation The Use of Earth Covered Buildings*, ed. Frank L. Moreland (Fort Worth, TX: National Science Foundation, 1975), 152–153.
6  See Alan H. Coogan, "Classification and Valuation of Subsurface Space," *Underground Space* 4 (1979): 175–186; Gavin J. Warnock, "New Frontiers of Inner Space-Underground★," *Underground Space* 1 (1978): 1–7.
7  Golany, *Earth-Sheltered Habitat*, 54–60.
8  Labs, "The Architectural Underground," 137.

**66** Novelty is but oblivion

9 Sydney A. Baggs, "A Taxonomy of Underground Space," in *Proceedings of the Earth Sheltered Housing Conference and Exhibition* (Minneapolis: University of Minnesota, 1980), 189–197.

10 Raymond L. Sterling, "Underground Space: Classifications and Configurations," in Carmody, and Sterling, *Underground Space Design*, 45–68.

11 See, as already told, Malcolm Wells, *Underground Designs*, Malcolm Wells, *Gentle Architecture*.

12 Kjed Vindum, "Eine Höhle für Jorn / A Cave for Jorn," *Daidalos* 48 (June, 1993): 65.

13 Yves Trinquesse, *Soleil en sous-sol* (Paris: Desforges, 1977), 81–86.

14 Piero Castiglioni, "Compiti visivi e riflessi psicologici dell'illuminazione artificiale," in *Proceedings of the Conference La città sotterranea nell'area Metropolitana* (Milan: Sindacato regionale ingegneri liberi professionisti della Lombardia, 1987), 83.

15 "With evening / the two or three colors of the patio grew weary. / Tonight, the moon's bright circle / does not dominate outer space. / Patio, heaven's watercourse. / The patio is the slope / down which the sky flows into the house. / Serenely / eternity waits at the crossway of the stars. / It is lovely to live in the dark friendliness / of covered entrance way, arbor, and wellhead." Jorge Luis Borges, "Patio," in *Selected Poems*, ed. Alexander Coleman (New York: Penguin, 2000), 15.

16 Golany, "Earth-Sheltered Habitat," 107.

17 It is estimated that energy saving compared to a traditional home, depending on the studies conducted and the areas in which it operates, passes from 23–35% to 70%. In Chris van Dronkelaar, Daniel Cóstola, Ritzki A. Mangkuto, and Jan L.M. Hensen, "Heating and cooling energy demand in underground buildings: Potential for saving in various climates and functions," *Energy and Buildings* 71 (December 2013): 129.

18 Samir Abdulak, and Pierre Pinon, "Maisons en pays islamique," *L'Architecture d'aujourd'hui* 167 (May–June 1973): 8.

19 Betsky, *Landscrapers: Building with the Land*, 2.

# 6
# STONE SKIES

Observing the development of housing from the 1940s onward, we are faced by two only apparently contrasting attitudes. Both approaches come from across the ocean, where local conditions are favorable and when changes in knowledge of construction or the arrival of new materials make it possible. On the one hand, houses become increasingly transparent, immersed in the landscape, even allowing the landscape itself to enter a box that is no longer made of masonry walls; on the other, there is the progressive dissolving of constructions, which foot after foot sink into the terrain.

While after World War II an era of democratic housing begins, at least on a typological level, the advertisements, tabloids and enormous billboards scattered along the highways of North America begin to impose new necessities with the advent of an invisible, cold and nerve-racking war: the need to seek underground shelter for protection against atomic fallout. At first they are just small outcroppings of the house – in backyard suburbia (Figure 6.1) – temporary havens connected to a hatch placed against the building or the barbecue, camouflaged by planters. In this period the pressure on public opinion plays a decisive role, with the mass media that continue to revive dystopian scenarios capable of altering the living habits of even the most incurable optimists.

Short films like *Atomic Power* or *One World or None* (1946),[1] movies like *The Beginning or the End* (1947), *The Atomic City* (1952) (Figure 6.2), all the way to reinterpretations from a certain distance in time like *The Atomic*

DOI: 10.4324/9781003214960-6

## 68 Stone skies

FIGURE 6.1   Entrance to a fallout shelter in the backyard, 1951 © Loomis Dean/The LIFE Picture Collection via Getty Images.

FIGURE 6.2   Poster for the film *The Atomic City* by Jerry Hopper, USA 1952.

*Café* (1982) or *Blast from the Past* (1999), give us a sense of how acutely the danger was perceived[2] and of what every true American could do – for himself or his country, to paraphrase Kennedy – in order to banish that danger. There was also the influence of television, which multiplied its sets from ten to over thirty million in the short span of four years, and the pressure of newspapers, magazines, tabloids, which can be summed up by the cover of *Life* with a man in a radiation suit and the headline "How You Can Survive Fallout," with the teasers "97 out of 100 people can be saved..." and "Detail plans for building shelters..."[3] Even comic books could not escape these latent fears, and the cover of the second issue of *Panic*, published by Tiny Tot Comics in May 1954, shows a boy exploding an atom bomb in the middle of a toy train set.[4]

With the rise in tensions between the superpowers, culminating first in the Bay of Pigs invasion and then in the Cuban Missile Crisis, specialized companies began to offer true survival cells, as prefabricated units to be buried or kits to construct on site. But these were still portions detached from the main dwelling, survival units for a limited period of time, and they were always dark places where no light could enter. The operation taken forward by Barnard, making him akin to an orthodox hypogean like Wells, is that of having rethought the house not in terms of refuge, but as a place in which to dwell for a lifetime.

It is no coincidence that the construction of the Ecology House took place before the oil crisis of 1973, though only slightly.[5] When OPEC cut back on production the price of crude oil tripled. The images of the time are not of the highest quality, but their contents are very clear: long lines at the gas pumps, fuel cans at the ready, abandoned service stations, early attempts to replace a primary resource like oil with alternative energy solutions.[6] Barnard's analysis began precisely from this aspect, inspired by principles of self-construction, cost reduction, energy savings: the first factor updated the pioneering tone of the early settlers, with drawings that convey an idea of the ease of construction by digging below ground level, and of the cell with two layers of wooden planks sandwiched around earth, or made with concrete blocks. The alternative was the insertion of a metal pipe such as those generally used for highway underpasses, closed at the ends by two bulkheads, placed halfway below the ground line with the other half covered by at least three feet of earth on all sides. Where rock and water prevented excavation, an open-air building was designed with gravel placed inside a dual layer of concrete blocks and covered by a concrete slab, gravel and earth, arranged as a lawn.[7] The word shared by the various solutions is "earth," which has the characteristic of being inexpensive and

## 70 Stone skies

the property of insulating a building not just from radiation but also from extremely hot or cold climates. This leads to the idea of a house that can reduce costs by 25% thanks to the materials and prefabrication, with fuel savings of 75% and without any need for external maintenance,[8] since it is a pure interior, an architecture of hollow space, a construction without facades (Figure 6.3).

The underground approach was certainly nothing new: in the end, one could look to historic examples like the complexes of homes in Tunisia, Turkey, China, though we do not know if Barnard was aware of Matmata, Cappadocia or the provinces of Honan, Shansi, Shensi and Kansu, since the systematic studies of this *modus abitandi* all came afterward.[9] Though his house was at a great geographical distance, with its location at Marston Mills, Massachusetts, the architect could not help but be aware of that area of the United States known as Four Corners – the meeting point of Utah, New Mexico, Arizona and Colorado – which due to climate conditions and the temporary settlement of nomads gave rise to the typology of the pit house,[10] a forerunner of the courtyard, patio or atrium house. Sometimes,

**FIGURE 6.3** John E. Barnard Jr., Ecology House, Osterville 1973 © Jack Lane.

Stone skies **71**

however, the aspirations, motivations and genesis of a model are simpler than one might imagine:

> I'd been fascinated with underground housing since I was a boy [...] My dad was an architect, and he would always say that if a house were deep enough in the earth, it would be sixty degrees all year round. So why not build houses down there? I mulled it over for a long time. My wife's response to trying an underground house was: 'I hope you and the mole you marry after I leave you will both be very happy.' Then, on a trip to Pompeii, we were sitting in a Romanesque[11] café with an atrium. And it dawned on me that if it were all dropped ten feet underground, you'd have the best of everything. My wife bought the idea; so I went ahead and built the house.[12]

The house is therefore a transposition in a modern key of a traditional type, and it exploits the same visual and climate modification mechanisms. Placed on three sides of an underground courtyard, it uses the fourth to insert the staircase (Figure 6.4). An apparently simple, almost banal arrangement, but one that based its design on precursory concepts such as the consumption of land in zones of high settlement density, energy savings and prevention of indiscriminate cutting of forests to produce timber.[13] From a visual standpoint, the courtyard is not a Leopardian limitation, but instead a precious source of privacy and at the same time a luminous backdrop for all the internal spaces, which are separated by glass walls, with the exception of the bathroom and the utility room. The twenty-eight square meters paved in stone permit use of the garden, which though surrounded by walls contains a tree at the center and a pool with a fountain placed below the staircase. This zone becomes a patio for sunbathing, conversation, dining, but also and above all for looking at the sky in a new way. The only signs of presence visible from the outside are the balustrade and the parking area. From a climate standpoint the courtyard is oriented towards the south, not only allowing all the rooms to receive sunlight even in the winter, but also functioning as a true heat exchanger capable of transforming the warm external space into a cool setting for use during most of the year.[14] The use of wood is reduced practically to zero, as Barnard himself explains:

> most homes built today have fairly low upkeep for the first ten or fifteen years on, [but then] a wood frame building requires a tremendous amount of exterior maintenance such as replacement of gutters, repainting and puttying, repairing termite damage, etc. If the

## 72 Stone skies

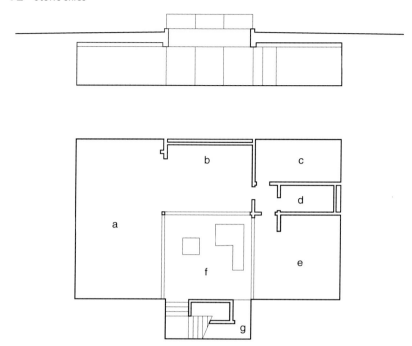

FIGURE 6.4 Plan and section: (a) living, (b) kitchen–dining, (c) service space, (d) bathroom, (e) bedroom, (f) patio, (g) storage.

homes were owner-built, this period of high expense generally coincides with time of retirement and decreased income. By omitting perishable materials from the exterior of the building and replacing them with glass, concrete and anodized aluminium this expense is eliminated.[15]

A house without an exterior, with walls in reinforced concrete properly insulated from the ground, with a roof in prefabricated panels topped by layers for waterproofing, insulation, drainage gravel and earth. Spare, essential furnishings reduced to the presence of armchairs and sofas in the living room (Figure 6.5); a work block, table and chairs in the kitchen, a bed and wardrobe in the bedroom. A prototype that judging from the information brochure that circulated that summer met with great success, since from July 1 to September 4 almost 10,000 people lined up to visit it.[16] The brochure, besides reporting on the above-mentioned economies,

Stone skies 73

**FIGURE 6.5** View of the courtyard from inside the living room © Jack Lane.

also underlined the house's virtues to stand up to storms and tornados, its resistance to fire and rotting, its versatility provided by a schema that could be applied to any type of lodging, office, school or apartment complex (Figure 6.6). It was not the first underground home to be built, but it had characteristics that set it apart from prototypes like the one presented by Jay Swayze at the New York World's Fair in 1964, the Winston House by Don Metz (1972), or the extensive earth-sheltered production of Malcolm Wells: all houses that were not really excavated, but covered with earth in keeping with the principle of "conservation architecture," namely a construction begun by man but completed by nature.

The fact that Barnard's house – already a symbol in its day – was disarmingly simple, as a home-manifesto, is demonstrated by the many emulations it gathered over the years. Not all are exact copies, though many are imitations, and others simply reproduce its essential features. They include the Earth House (Figure 6.7)[17] in Yangpyeong-gun County, in the South Korean province of Gyeonggi-do: built by BCHO Architects in 2008–2009, it takes its cue from the poet Yoon Dong-joo, author of verses on the theme of the earth, sky and stars, to create a sort of large window

**74** Stone skies

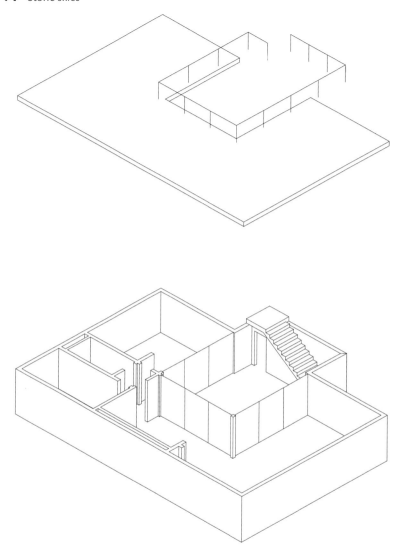

**FIGURE 6.6** Isometric.

whose frames are the perimeter walls of an underground courtyard. The building faces outward on just two sides, which are moreover opposite each other, and the staircase also differs, as it is placed outside the perimeter of the construction (Figure 6.8). While the one took all the light from the outside, in keeping with the climate, the other has small openings that face onto the square open space and onto an opening in the roof that

**FIGURE 6.7** View of the Earth House by BCHO Architects, Jipyeong-myeon, 2008-09 © Wooseop Hwang.

contains the bedrooms at the back. Instead of seeking light, the design offers shelter from the sun, also thanks to an inclined canopy placed to protect the entrance doors (Figure 6.9). Thanks to its different orientation the house takes advantage of passive cooling, and a network of geothermal pipes makes it possible to keep the dwelling cool in summer and warm in winter. The house is camouflaged only from a distance because the roof is left exposed, and the interior with small rooms separated by dividers in rammed earth, without any trace of glass or transparency, also differs. A work of *Terratektur* based on the principle of sustainability, implying the use of material taken from the excavation, but also following the local construction tradition that calls for very small rooms, in tune with the structure that supports them (Figure 6.10).

Getting back to 885 Race Lane, this villa presents several constants that go well beyond the individual work. First of all, the ability to adapt the typology to different climates and types of terrain: located in Barnstable County, it indicated a sort of underground International Style, avoiding the occupation of the various contexts with the same type of architecture and safeguarding the different existing landscapes by removing itself from view. All this without having a passive approach, subjected to the context, but as an opportunity for a more appealing view with respect to the

**76** Stone skies

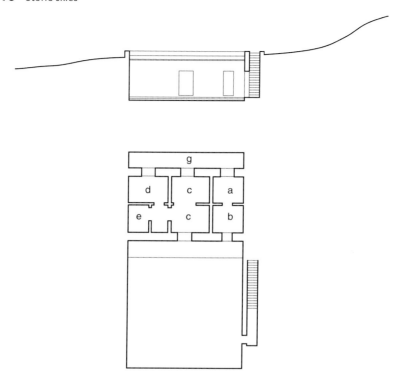

**FIGURE 6.8** Plan and section: (a) studio, (b) kitchen, (c) bedroom, (d) bathroom, (e) laundry room, (f) patio, (g) courtyard.

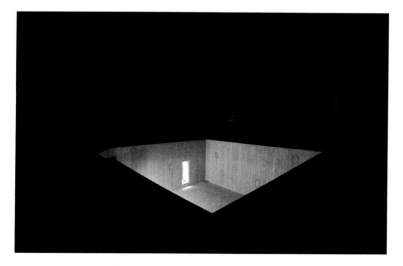

**FIGURE 6.9** Nocturnal view of the courtyard, © Wooseop Hwang.

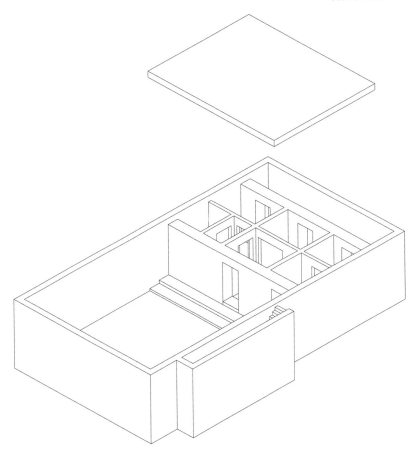

**FIGURE 6.10** Isometric.

urban or suburban panorama composed of clotheslines, trash cans, traffic and commerce. Secondly, it is a concealment without standardization. The lack of distinction from the other houses through traditional systems of facade composition in no way implies a lack of recognizability, just as "sinking" into the terrain does not imply a multiplicity of houses around a courtyard, as still happens today in many "cave-dwelling" populations, but a singularity that can be repeated, endlessly modified, never equal to itself.

Finally, there is the idea of the replacement of the solid sky cherished by Calvino with a ceiling of stars. We thus pass from "a stone sky [that] rotated above our heads, one more limpid than yours"[18] to "a room that no longer has walls […] this violet ceiling / no longer exists. / I see the sky above

**78** Stone skies

us."[19] On the one hand the imagined transparency made of many layers,[20] and on the other real, true transparency, to "touch" with one's hand. A thought that in the past obsessed entire ranks of master builders, architects, engineers with the correspondence between celestial and ceiling, with the flatness of the term soffit that came before the concept of the vault. Just consider the many cathedrals, churches, chapels whose vaults have been painted with a blue background on which golden stars stood out. "It may be said that at great periods of architecture ceilings were always skies."[21] The next step came with ateliers of painters, the *passages*, the galleries, the large surfaces that have placed glass between us and the sky, but Barnard's work certainly makes a leap of quality, with the emptiness that intervenes, exposing us as Wordsworth would say to "Infinity's embrace."[22]

## Notes

1  Many of these "docufictions" were funded directly by the United States through various government agencies.
2  Michael Scheibach, *Atomic Narratives and American Youth: Coming of Age with the Atom, 1945–1955* (Jefferson, NC and London: McFarland & Company, 2003).
3  The main article was preceded by a letter from the then President John Fitzgerald Kennedy.
4  Scheibach, *Atomic Narratives and American Youth*, 164–165.
5  The house was built between the winter of 1972 and the spring of 1973.
6  In addition to photos of newspapers and magazines of the time, see the beautiful images contained in Giovanna Borasi, and Mirko Zardini, eds., *Sorry, Out of Gas: Architecture's Response to the 1973 Oil Crisis* (Montréal and Mantova: Canadian Centre for Architecture-Corraini, 2007).
7  Shel Hershorn, Dimitri Kessel, Francis Miller, Ralph Morse, and Eric Schall, eds., "Fallout Shelters. You could be among the 97% to survive if you follow on these pages... How to build shelters... where to hide in cities... what to do during an attack," *Life* 11 (September 15, 1961): 95–108.
8  John E. Barnard, ed., *Ecology House*, undated brochure. See Kaiman Lee, ed., *Encyclopedia of Energy-efficient Building Design: 391 Practical Case Studies* (Boston, MA: Environmental Design and Research Center, 1977), 352.
9  Labs, "The Architectural Underground," 1–8, 135–156; Sydney A. Baggs, "A Taxonomy of Underground Space," 189–197; Gideon Golany, *Earth-Sheltered Habitat: History, Architecture and Urban Design* (New York: Van Nostrand Reinhold, 1983). In fact, in an interview he says: "I read recently of an entire village in north China built underground." In John E. Barnard, "A New Life – Underground," *Wentworth Institute Bulletin* 8 (October 1973): 10.
10  Kempe, *Living Underground*, 104–110.
11  Obviously, Barnard meant Roman and not Romanesque. Some, like Labs, refer directly to the underground houses of Bulla Regia.
12  Mike Edelhart, "The Food Life Underground," *Omni* 4 (January 1980): 55.
13  "Saving by Going Underground," *AIA Journal* 61 (February 1974): 48–49.

14 Ali A. Al-Temeemi, and Doug J. Harris, "A Guideline for Assessing the Suitability of Earth-Sheltered Mass-Housing in Hot-Arid Climates," *Energy and Buildings* 36 (March 2004): 251–260.

15 Barnard, ed., *Ecology House*, n.p.

16 William J. Lanouette, "Architect Sinks to New Depths and Digs It," *Chicago Tribune*, February 8, 1975.

17 See Matteo Vercelloni, "Earth House, Gyeonggi-do, South Korea (Byoungsoo Cho and others)," *Casabella* 799 (March 2011): 27–30.

18 Italo Calvino, "The Stone Sky," in Italo Calvino, *The Complete Cosmicomics* (Boston, MA: Houghton Mifflin Hartcourt Jonathan, 2014), 333.

19 Some verses from *Il cielo in una stanza* written by Gino Paoli in 1960.

20 "We knew that the Earth is made up of superimposed roofs, like the skins of an enormous onion, and that every roof leads you to a roof higher up, and all of them together prefigure the final roof, the point where the Earth ceases to be Earth, where all the inside is left on this side, and beyond there is only the outside." In Calvino, "The Stone Sky," 334–335.

21 William R. Lethaby, *Architecture, Mysticism and Myth* (New York: Dover, 1891), 222.

22 William Wordsworth, "Inside of King's College Chapel, Cambridge: Continued," in *The Poetical Works* (London: Longman, Rees, Orme, Brown & Green, 1827), 3: 442.

# 7
## SENSATIONS

My hair stood on end, my teeth chattered, my limbs trembled. […] Decidedly, I hadn't had enough 'lessons in chasms' at the Vor Frelsers Kirke in Copenhagen.

These are the words of the most famous imaginative explorer in all of literature, Jules Verne, who though he never walked the descending path of the Snæfell volcano was quite capable of conveying the sense of discomfort felt by many when they go down into the bowels of the earth. Sensations such as that of the cold, which in terms of actual weather conditions had no scientific basis. The underground space, even in areas lashed by the frigid winds of the north, or as we have seen in the torrid conditions of the Tunisian desert, has always been synonymous with protection, shelter, defense. The novelist, rather like what Emilio Salgari would do at the start of the 20th century, simply displayed what the reader was expecting to see and hear. Actually, from a strictly biological standpoint, entering and spending time in a subterranean habitat, due to its environmental characteristics, helps to regulate the nervous system, maintaining the production and release of body heat, stimulating metabolic rates and resistance to illness,[1] and thus represents − at least over the short term − a sort of optimal condition. Constant temperature and stable relative humidity even have the effect of increasing longevity, as confirmed by analyses conducted on the populations of certain regions in China.[2]

DOI: 10.4324/9781003214960-7

This effect of thermoregulation adapts to both cold-humid and hot-arid climates, as can be seen in Australia in towns like Coober Pedy (Figure 7.1) and White Cliffs (Figure 7.2). In the latter, a small population has lived in caves for over a century, thanks to the ability to lower external temperature by twenty degrees, depending on the cross-section, the depth of the construction and the type of ventilation utilized.[3]

The states of New South Wales and South Australia represent yet another demonstration of the fact that the use of excavation and of the earth's crust as a layer inside which to dwell knows no geographical boundaries. The data show that these settlements act as true "regulators" of the main factors governing thermo-hygrometric comfort, putting the shape of the cavity – heights and depths – in relation to the internal parameters. In particular, in the Victoria area, the caves originally inhabited by aboriginal people in the settlements of East Buchan and Mount Eccles show that in the type created from a slope with a single opening for access, the wet-bulb and dry-bulb temperature drops drastically once past the entrance: in these examples the interface between internal and external space makes use of expedients to minimize the exchange between the two environments,

**FIGURE 7.1** Landscape at Coober Pedy in the state of South Australia, Australia © M.T. Shaw.

**82** Sensations

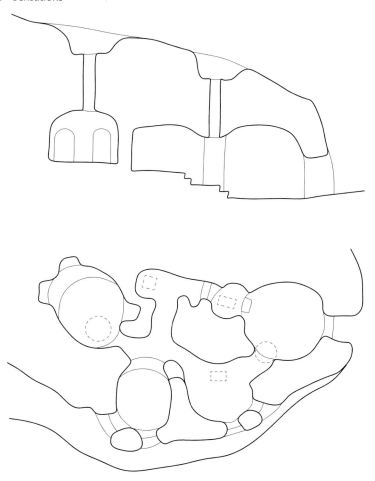

**FIGURE 7.2** Plan and section of an excavated dwelling with aeration at White Cliffs, in the state of New South Wales, Australia.

such as the compression of the entrance in the first case or even the descent by way of a staircase to a lower level, in the second.[4]

The ground is therefore an enormous potential resource for energy saving, and this is simply because starting from the last Ice Age the Earth has been incessantly subjected to the warming action of the sun's rays, to the point of bringing it to a semi-static thermal condition.[5] Studies conducted in recent decades agree that the percentage of savings with respect to an above-ground work may vary from 47% to 80% depending on the type of terrain, to 33–50–70% depending on the function of the construction. In any case, comparing the same typology made above or under ground, the function of a building with the highest level of reduction of energy requirements is that of housing, industry or offices, with savings of as much as 60–70%, as opposed to 25–40% for the sectors of education, healthcare and sports.[6] These results are not very different from those hypothesized by John Barnard Jr. just forty years earlier.[7]

These estimates that link the use of buildings to obtainable energy savings are partially subject to revision if we take the internal heat gain of the different functions and surrounding conditions imposed by the climate of their location into consideration. This premise can be translated into a ranking summed up by the principle according to which the architectures that contain functions with low heat gain, as in the case of residential buildings, are underground types best optimized in warm climates, while functions that involve a large number of users, such as those for sporting activities, lead to better results in cool climates.[8]

While as we have seen the type of placement is decisive, the type of terrain is no less important. It is no coincidence that the largest number of people living in underground dwellings is found in China, where the *loess* – a loamy deposit formed by wind, of glacial origin, in which it is easy to dig thanks to its lack of hardness and its high porosity – constitutes the best possible construction material. The same kind of favorable context exists in the already cited example of Matmata, in which the ease of working on the site represented the indispensable condition for its settlement, considering the limited tools for excavation of the cave dwellers that founded the village. With the passing centuries the malleability of the materials becomes less important, thanks to technological progress and to the priority placed on guarantees of insulation and structural performance in architecture today. Precisely the level of heat on the ground, together with the geomorphological conditions of the site, are among the aspects that influence the initial choice of the location and the behavior of the structure: in a city like Shanghai variation curves can be obtained between three and seven degrees in summer and one and seven degrees in winter. Likewise, the data of the walls of an underground construction reflect the condition of the immediately adjacent areas, following the temperature distribution gradient from the warmer surface layers to the deeper layers, already stabilizing at approximately three meters of depth.[9]

Taking an empirical approach that overlooks the different variables impacting the conditions of the terrain, in temperate climates the behavior can be summed up in three phases. On the basis of depth increment it is

**84** Sensations

possible to already detect an attenuation of 20% at ten centimeters from the surface with respect to the variation of air heat, with a phase shift of six hours. Below thirty centimeters the daily variation of external temperature is completely absorbed by the thermal inertia of the ground. Reaching a depth of five meters, we can measure a constant condition equal to the annual average of the location, with a deviation of the order of one degree centigrade.[10] This exponential reduction of the external thermal variation and of the temperature in general evens out the performance of an underground building in various periods of the year. This observation is equally important if we consider it from an opposite standpoint, namely that of the dispersion of heat from an underground space towards the outside. The achievement of comfort in an underground situation happens both in the warm period and the cool period, given the proximity of the maximum dispersions to the average dispersions of the building.

The combination of limited dispersion and inertia of the terrain with respect to the external climate – a formula that puts the underground condition into a position of advantage in terms of energy consumption – is joined by the concept of PAHS, passive annual heat storage, i.e. the capacity to exploit these characteristics in order to further increase the performance of a building on an annual basis. PAHS is a method used to accumulate heat during the summer through natural cooling and storage of the heat in the ground itself, which will release it to the building through shared surfaces during the winter.[11] The strategy is fundamentally based on the thermodynamic principle by which heat flows naturally from a warmer object to a cooler object. In other words, the ground contains the possibility of regulating temperature in architecture, a sort of *deus ex machina ante litteram*, prior to the use of machines to heat or cool water and air.

To assess the benefits of an underground location for a basic shelter, we can identify two volume types – one partially inserted in a hillside (slope design), the other completely below ground, like a courtyard (atrium design) – in which it becomes clear not only that PAHS and passive cooling strategies can be enormously advantageous in both summer and winter, but also that this advantage is maximized by the patio typology.[12] Therefore the form can also have an impact on living conditions and, to paraphrase Sullivan, form follows *climate*. In warm zones the best form is that of the rectangle, or one with the largest possible number of sides, because the greater the surface exposed to the ground, the greater the thermal exchange, leading to more efficient cooling of the spaces. Vice versa, in cooler zones the circular form, or in general a form with less exposed surface, reduces heat dispersion – hence the trend towards compact dwellings.[13]

Besides all these considerations, there is obviously also the contribution offered to underground architecture by natural ventilation.

The difference of temperature inside and outside the building, though reduced to a minimum by the action of the terrain, in any case permits a fundamental phenomenon of aeration, which if suitably designed and controlled can become a further factor for savings in the overall energy consumption of an underground shelter.

> The mouth of the Cave us'd to fend forth a gentle murmuring sound, and that too by Intervals, as if by its frequent sighs its jaws were now shut, and now open'd; hence the Literati of Bergen [...] excited the younger inhabitants to a closer examination of the nature of the cavern; especially as a stated intervals, after the manner of human respiration, the sound being sometime with-held issued out with a certain proportional force.[14]

The tale told by Niels Klim (Figure 7.3), but also historic examples like the houses of Jerusalem or the dwellings of ancient Mesopotamia allow us to observe how the ground mass, while preventing heat dispersion, also blocks the passage of air at the same time, which thus has to take place through controlled openings. The quantity and quality of the gaps are variables firmly linked to the design, which can take on the characteristics of cross or ascensional ventilation, and all the conditions found in traditional architecture. The passage and circulation of air constitute one of the basic conditions of everyday experience of architecture, from the times in which casements did not exist, all the way to the practice of aerating homes based on the path of the sun, before the introduction of air conditioning. It comes naturally, from the outset, to point to a limitation of good passive ventilation, namely the fact that a building partially or completely below ground has less possibility of opening to the outside, and therefore has few ways to be crossed, which in any case are reduced to the use of windows and chimneys. This observable drawback, however, is abundantly compensated by the benefits offered by the underground context to increase internal wellbeing.

Taking warm, dry climates as a typical case, namely situations requiring more circulation of air, it is interesting to understand how it can be treated like a fluid to manipulate and channel through intakes on the ground surface, deviations and compressions, all tools that have to come to terms with the morphological characteristics of the site and its wind conditions. The approach involves a kind of track on which to control this flow, without

## 86 Sensations

**FIGURE 7.3** Etching by Johan Frederik Clemens, from a drawing by Nicolai Abildgaard, depicting Niels Klim, Copenhagen 1789.

direct exposure to the wind which often brings with it dust and debris. The difference in conception between buildings constructed on a slope and those organized around a courtyard lies precisely in the routes that can be plotted, all aimed at a constant flow in the interiors, always as an optimized fraction of the currents on the ground surface (Figure 7.4).

Very specific dynamics can be seen in the above-mentioned cases at Coober Pedy, where conduits excavated in a way that resembles the intricate dynamism of mines represent a solution that exploits the chimney effect, facilitating air circulation (Figure 7.5). The pressure differential created thanks to the underground situation triggers utterly exceptional internal movements, which can be manifested on the surface as blasts of air,[15] a sort of Icelandic *mistour* to link back to Verne's narrative. These puffs, made visible by the sand of the Australian landscapes, are the result of skillful channeling designed for this purpose with diagrams that show the relationship between air speed and ground level. Not only are these factors

Sensations **87**

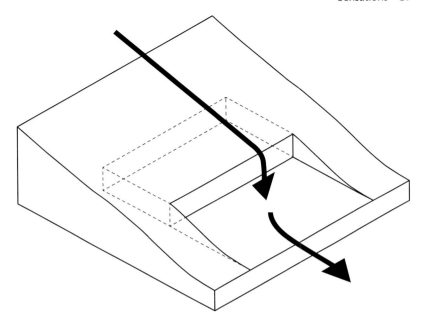

**FIGURE 7.4**  Ventilation in a hillside house.

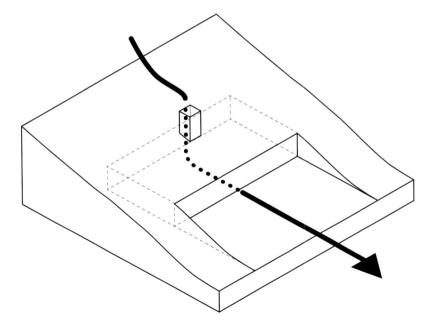

**FIGURE 7.5**  Ventilation in a hillside house with chimney.

## 88 Sensations

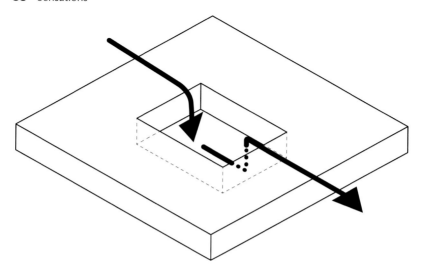

**FIGURE 7.6** Ventilation in a plains house with patio.

directly proportional, we can also observe a rise in ventilation in keeping with the depth of the excavation (Figure 7.6).[16]

While elaborate but rudimentary conduits wind under the sands of the Southern Hemisphere, much more complex devices are found in the wind towers of Iran. Authentic monuments to the air, standing out like obelisks at the corners of constructions, these towers give rise to a system of natural mechanical circulation that dates back tens of centuries prior to contemporary energy saving protocols. These devices call for the burial of air collectors to channel ventilation towards the various rooms, served by chimneys oriented on the prevailing wind direction (Figure 7.7). The cross-section of these volumes is divided into two equal parts, one for the entry of air, the other to expel it after its circulation inside the building. The writer H.G. Wells also understood the importance of these systems of capture and expulsion of air (Figure 7.8):

> A peculiar feature that presently attracted my attention was certain circular wells that appeared to sink to a profound depth. One lay by the path up the hill which I had followed during my first walk. […] Sitting by the side of these, and peering down, I failed to see any gleam of water, and could catch no reflection from a lighted match. […] I discovered from the flaring of the match that a steady

Sensations **89**

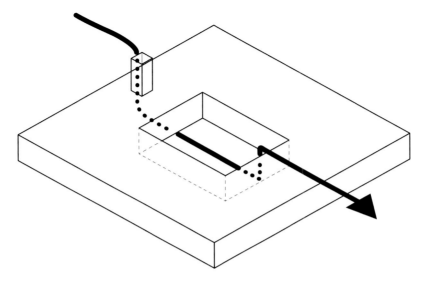

**FIGURE 7.7**  Ventilation in a plains house with patio and chimney.

**FIGURE 7.8**  Ventilation wells in a still taken from *The Time Machine*, by George Pal, USA 1960.

current of air set down the shaft. Moreover, I carelessly threw a scrap of paper into the throat of the well, and instead of fluttering slowly down, it was at once sucked swiftly out of sight. After a time, too, I came to connect with these wells certain tall towers that stood here

FIGURE 7.9  Drone's-eye view of the SRMS & A house by Werner Tscholl, Castelbello (BZ) 2014–2017 © Albrecht Auer (Staschitz).

and there upon the hill slopes. Above these there was often apparent a peculiar flicker of the air, much as one sees it on a hot day above a sun-scorched beach. Putting these things together there certainly seemed to me a strong suggestion of an extensive system of subterraneous ventilation.[17]

The approach to ventilation somehow recapitulates the difference that exists between methods we might define as "erosive" and those that are constructive: the former, spontaneous in character, exploit natural cavities using archaic means – excavation of niches, passages, enlargements and conduits – while the latter, which some might define as cultured,[18] deploy contemporary technologies. Actually, another path also exists, which can be seen in works like the SRMS & A house by Werner Tscholl at Castelbello in Trentino-Alto Adige (Figure 7.9). Here the methods are mixed and combined, avoiding the rhetoric of the ecological approach in favor of a sort of cavern *sub specie machinae* (Figures 7.10 and 7.11). The cliff dwelling becomes a "concrete-sheltered house" that literally penetrates into the stone; a house that time will conceal from view when the roof begins to be covered with moss, thanks to the treatment of the surface roughened by the hand finishing done with spades, rakes and brooms.[19] A thin shell

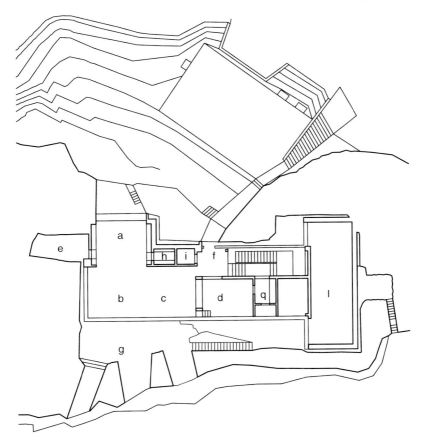

**FIGURE 7.10** Ground floor plan: (a) kitchen, (b) dining room, (c) living area, (d) studio, (e) cellar, (f) entrance, (g) terrace, (h) closet, (i) elevator, (l) void, (m) garage, (o) sauna, (p) bedroom (q) bathroom, (r) courtyard.

resting on pillars and partitions, suspended at times, filled in with glass panels (Figure 7.12) that not only permit constant contact with the rock and the view of the valley, but also provide cross ventilation, first through the walls and then upward. A volume initially incised, then subtracted from the bulk of the mountain and finally returned to it in the form of a tent stretched amidst compact rocks, steep cliffs and ravines (Figure 7.13).

A dialogue with the existing context that is not aimed at compliance with the local language of construction, but takes part in the aerial life

**92** Sensations

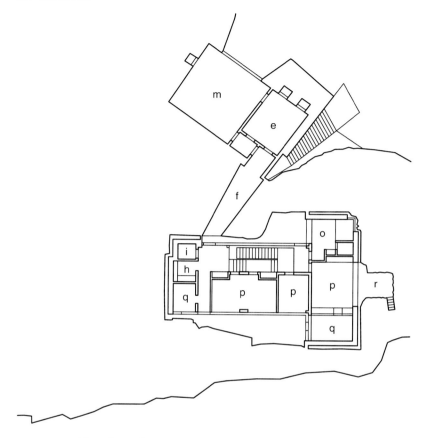

**FIGURE 7.11** First floor plan: (a) kitchen, (b) dining room, (c) living area, (d) studio, (e) cellar, (f) entrance, (g) terrace, (h) closet, (i) elevator, (l) void, (m) garage, (o) sauna, (p) bedroom, (q) bathroom, (r) courtyard.

of the mountain, letting itself be transported by a game of references between underlying forms and landscapes, and finally abandoning itself to the diaphanous glow of the sun's rays. Here the lithic memory of the site is understood, grasping the importance of light, and here we can fully comprehend the lesson of the chasm.

**FIGURE 7.12** The southern facade and the terrace © René Riller.

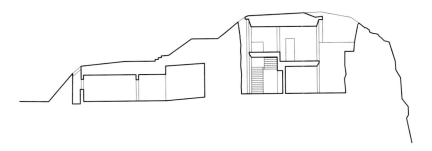

**FIGURE 7.13** Cross-section of the house.

## Notes

1 Gideon Golany, and Toshio Ojima, *Geo-Space Urban Design* (New York: Wiley & Sons, 1996), 67. Obviously living underground, which includes alternation of indoor and outdoor, mustn't be confused with the extreme experiments of stays in caves for long periods, which have, as told before, different consequences on health.
2 Huo Yan, "The Effects of Cave Dwelling on Human Health," *Tunnelling and Underground Space Technology* 2 (1986): 171–175.

**94** Sensations

3 Sydney A. Baggs, "The dugout Dwellings of an Outback Opal Mining Town in Australia," in *Underground Utilization: A Reference Manual of Selected Works*, ed. Truman Stauffer (Kansas City: University of Missouri, 1978), 573–599.

4 Ibid., 581.

5 Sydney A. Baggs, "Underground Earth-Insulated Architecture," *Building Economist* 16 (June 1977): 17.

6 van Dronkelaar, Cóstola, Mangkuto, and Hensen, "Heating and cooling energy demand in underground buildings: Potential for savings in various climates and functions," 129, 134.

7 Barnard is quoted in particular in Elaine V. Smay, "Underground Houses-Low Fuel Bills, Low Maintenance, Privacy, Security," *Popular Science* 4 (April 1977): 84–89, 155.

8 Van Dronkelaar, Cóstola, Mangkuto, and Hensen, "Heating and Cooling Energy Demand in Underground Buildings: Potential for Savings in Various Climates and Functions," 134.

9 Hou Xueyuan, and Su Yu, "The Urban Underground Space Environment and Human Performance," *Tunnelling and Underground Space Technology* 2 (1988): 195–196.

10 Walter F. Spiegel, "Air Quality and Heat Transfer," in *The Use of Earth Covered Buildings. In Proceedings of the Conference Alternatives in Energy Conservation*, ed. Frank L. Moreland (Fort Worth, TX: National Science Foundation, 1975), 248.

11 The basic concept of PAHS is by John N. Hait, *Passive Annual Heat Storage: Improving the Design of Earth Shelters, or, How to Store Summer's Sunshine to Keep your Wigwam Warm all Winter* (Missoula, MT: Rocky Mountain Research Center, 1983). See also Akubue Jideofor Anselm, "Passive Annual Heat Storage Principles in Earth Sheltered Housing, a Supplementary Energy Saving System in Residential Housing," *Energy and Buildings* 40 (July 2008): 1214–1219.

12 Akubue J. Anselm, "Earth Shelters. A Review of Energy Conservation Properties in Earth Sheltered Housing," in *Energy Conservation*, ed. Azni Zain Ahmed (Rijeka: Intech, 2012), 125–148.

13 Golany, *Earth-Sheltered Habitat*, 105–108.

14 Ludvig Holberg, *A Journey to the World Under-Ground* (London: T. Astley and B. Collins, 1742), 3.

15 Baggs, "The dugout Dwellings of an Outback Opal Mining Town in Australia," 587–588.

16 Ibid., 590.

17 Herbert George Wells, *The Time Machine* (New York: Henry Holt & Co., 1895), 93–94.

18 Manfredi Nicoletti, *L'architettura delle caverne* (Rome: Laterza, 1980), 11–12.

19 Marco Mulazzani, "Werner Tscholl, Casa SMRS & A, Castelbello, Bolzano," *Casabella* 886 (June 2018): 102. See also Werner Tscholl, "Hábitat Troglodita, House SMRS &A, Castelbello (Italy)," *Arquitectura Viva* 209 (November 2018): 32–35.

# 8
# SOUS PASSAGES

"The interior […], for the private man, represents the universe. In the interior, he brings together the far away and the long ago. His living room is a box in the theater of the world."[1] The *interieur*, a sort of constellation of parallel, artificial, constructed worlds, forms the seamless lining of man's architecture, representing an important piece of that continuum of fragments utilized by Benjamin to describe the dynamics of 19th-century Paris. The setup of these places, contextualized in the modern era, and thus in an already advanced stage of contemporary consumption, can fit the maxim that contrasts a global interior and a local exterior.[2] To be definitively inside is a sensation of being sheltered from the *open field* of the world (Figure 8.1), which is also closely connected – once across the exit threshold – to the image of the city to which it belongs. But how could we define these relations, were we to pass from these "shelters" to underground interiors, were we to literally plunge into these spaces below ground level? We would find ourselves faced with an architecture of enclosed spaces that has not only forgotten cultural areas, regionalisms and local languages, but is also unable to establish a relationship with a landscape connected to a specific context, due to its subterranean nature. Furthermore, the *intérieur* in this case is often associated with the concept of direction, transformed into directional space[3]: an evolution that becomes segment and movement, presenting itself as a channel of connection between two distant poles, a bridge between concepts that we usually attribute to the underpass.

DOI: 10.4324/9781003214960-8

## Sous passages

**FIGURE 8.1** Benthem Crouwel Architects, Cuyperspassage, Amsterdam 2015 © Jannes Linders.

With the same diachronic approach we have applied to interiors, we can compare this type of architectural device with those from which Benjamin took the name of his unfinished work. Starting from the conception of the *passage* itself (Figure 8.2), inseparable from Paris which witnessed its rise and fall, it is clear that it is hard to find a place of origin in the collective imagination for its underground brethren, the sub-passages, the underpasses. In an opposite and almost symmetrical way, these place themselves in a condition of otherness – indifferent counterpoint of identity – capable only of bringing to mind the atmosphere and the internal dynamics, without a memory of substrate, or a specific context of belonging. The sub-passages whose genetic background we are attempting to decipher are orphans and offspring of all, so anonymous in their construction as to leave no doubt regarding their utilitarian approach as a connection between distinct points. Their use is incessantly repeated without demands, without feeling any unfulfilled expectation, any architectural thought during the moment of crossing.

How could we fail to insert them in the ranks of the "non-places" that govern the dilation of our urban landscapes,[4] necessary evils or assets not sufficiently necessary to deserve attention, attribution of value and resources? They can be considered, in short, on a par with prepared foods

**FIGURE 8.2** Present-day view of Passage Jouffroy, Paris 1846 © Antonello Boschi.

ready for a quick lunch during a frenetic day of work. An architectural lobotomy,[5] which not only establishes relations between container and content, but also totally conceals the first under the surface of the world, and the second behind a suspension of judgment that has more to do with the lack of alternatives than with an indifference of perception.

The underpass, observed from a perspective that sees it as a tool to address the need for connections between city parts, between underground means of communication or between uncrossable barriers at ground level, and not as the objective of an everyday experience, owes this status to a large extent to what we might define as its habitual passerby.

"Landscape – that, in fact, is what Paris becomes for the *flâneur*. Or, more precisely: the city splits for him into its dialectical poles. It opens up to him as a landscape, even as it closes around him as a room."[6] So the great corridors of the *passages* – ideal syncretism of landscape and room – would not have had the same charm had it not been for the figures who distractedly walked through them: figures that suggested the incessant wandering, the sporadic and winding steps typical of those who have no destination in particular. While the *flâneur* can represent the animate expression of the

**98** Sous passages

Parisian *passage*, it would be hard to outline the features of his underground alter ego of our time. By induction, we can try to describe some of his salient characteristics. The gait: taut, quick, attentive, suitable for places where it is better to keep moving, on the way to elsewhere. The gaze: low, steady, almost catatonic, watching the ground beneath one's steps, while paying fleeting attention to the screen of a smartphone. The listening: little interaction with others, a capacity often replaced by the multimedia content provided by the above-mentioned device that draws the gaze. There are pathways of the gaze[7] that resemble the agitated and jerky ones of someone driving in traffic more than those described by Walser[8] of a writer lost in his thoughts, in search of inspiration. These characteristics are antithetical to those we might mention for a person walking on ground level, perhaps enjoying time thus spent on a beautiful sunny day. In these terms, the underpass can be considered an effective heterotopia[9] of the walk, a conveyor of fluxes that triggers a short circuit in man's capacity to appreciate the environment around him and to weave relationships inside it. To use an analogy with the dynamics of mining, where the branching tunnels are channels of extraction and at the same time the result of this activity, the underpasses are instead places of insertion, of constant movement. A quick pace, as in *Modern Times*, underscored by eloquent suggestions like the famous "keep left" scattered in the London Underground to urge "slow" travelers to leave the passing lane free. This movement of millions brings to mind the unstoppable progress of Pac-Man (Figure 8.3), the historic video game in which the protagonist gobbles up flashing dots of light along an obligatory maze, escaping from monsters we might call time, work and routine today.

It is precisely the metropolitan system as we know it today, a constant in all big cities, that feeds on underpasses not only to descend towards trains, but also to weave a network of connections between one station and another, or between different lines in the same station. Recalling the psychogeography theorized by Debord and the Situationist movement,[10] in these dark connections between city pieces we can rediscover the dynamics evoked inside the Naked City (Figure 8.4). In an imaginary representation of the city, nineteen sections of Paris were taken apart by the French philosopher and reassembled in a new order. The arrows that connect them can be compared to those underground pathways that represent a break in our location inside the city, inside the cardinal points and under the vault of the sky. This multisensory suspension of perception is the real dystopia of the "dérives" (drifts) theorized by the Situationists, who urged people to "…walk rhythmically and look slightly upwards, so that architecture will be the center of your visual field, and leave the street level at the lower end of your sight."[11]

Sous passages **99**

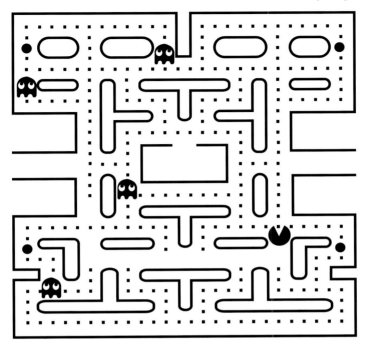

**FIGURE 8.3** *Pac-Man*, typical scheme of the famous video game, 1980.

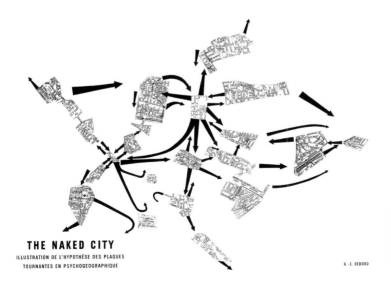

**FIGURE 8.4** Guy Debord, *Naked City*, 1957 © Frac-Val de Loire.

Beyond these digressions that take their dynamic nature as a constant of passages, we should remember that "corridors no longer simply link A to B, but have become 'destinations.'"[12] We cannot say the same, with comparable nonchalance, about underpasses, apart from some specific episodes that have to do with the subculture known (not by chance) as "underground." Part of this subculture, almost never dazzled by the poetic instant of Bachelard, makes graffiti that have something in common with the signs described by Venturi almost fifty years ago in his famous *Learning from Las Vegas*.[13] In this logic, not only do the importance and size of the works seem to be directly proportional to each other, but the superimposing of one work on another represents a sort of stratification that asserts one work by obliterating the one that came before it. The "writers," surrogates of protest movements whose legacy they seem to carry on, take possession of underpasses and other places in the city associated with darkness and night, as the not just physical but also communicative setting for the propagation of their personal "tags" in a sort of obsessive-compulsive formula (Figure 8.5). The phenomenon, which reaches its climax in "tag bombing,"[14] represents a form of control of the territory and of resistance to the canons of the society that every day, in those sub-passages, "looks and passes." This

**FIGURE 8.5** Tag bombing in a subway, Belfast © Antonello Boschi.

practice seems to reveal a veiled abandonment syndrome more than an atrocious act of revolt, contributing above all, though not on its own, to mark these as violated, inhospitable places. Alongside the presence of these denizens, we cannot fail to mention the use of underground passages as shelters for the homeless,[15] nestled at their sides to spend the night inside something, a memory of architecture that can protect them without expulsion. A consideration that with some exaggeration can also have to do with the *pissoirs* of Paris – placed like punctuation at the corners of the streets – in relation to a blurry free zone of underpasses, potential linear urinals we are accustomed to encountering at the rest stops along our highways.

To round out the dark, dramatic image the mind associates with these spaces, often boosted by news reports, we can think about one of the first works of Kieślowski,[16] *Pedestrian Subway* (Figure 8.6), where an act of sexual violence takes place. In a setting where everyone passes through and no one remains, the rules established for itself by the society vanish due to the lack of the indirect control the community exerts over the territory, on a par with the mechanism described by Jane Jacobs regarding the difference between old cities and new turf.[17]

**FIGURE 8.6** Still taken from *Przejście podziemne* (Pedestrian Subway) by Krysztof Kieślowski, Poland 1973.

**102** Sous passages

Bringing back to mind the impact of the will-o'-the-wisps of the *passages* on Benjamin's imaginary, we can recall that "these corridors are massive works of architecture in marble, glass and iron, soon to become obsolete, like the buildings of the first factories, and therefore they contain something dreamy, unredeemed, of childhood memory."[18] Parallel to this vision, in the underpasses we can rediscover another side of our subconscious linked to the hidden and invisible dimension of the world. Man has always deposited and concealed his fears below the ground, but also the expectations connected with life after death, and other rituals that find a physical and symbolic passage from darkness to light in the descent-ascent dichotomy. One significant example is linked to the god Zeus Idaios in Pre-Mycenaean Crete: "The rite foresaw that the initiate [...] would then go down into the darkness of the tomb-cave of god. At dawn of the twenty-eighth day, they would return to the light."[19] Here the underground passage represented a destination, albeit temporary, the sole path of contact with the divine. Without recourse to western cosmogony, it is possible to outline an aesthetic of the underpass, coming to grips with its relationship with light and space to dredge up the origin and dynamics that influence our forebodings when we enter its depths. The first factor has to do with the use of artificial light, an inevitable device that often cannot be combined with direct or diffused sunlight. The second is generated by following a hedonistic principle, i.e. limiting the size of these passages in order to cut down on the costs of excavation and construction. A dynamic that reminds us of the burrows of certain animals, marmots, badgers, rabbits. Tunnels for shelter inside the warm womb of mother earth, generated by removal, in keeping with a spatial configuration barely sufficient to create an inhabitable space.

The logic underlying the *Existenzminimum* of these excavations is "deeply" different from the foundation logic of the *passages*, based on the vision of a light showcase to contain a portion of the city. The will to enclose the consumer – once the citizen – inside a glass bubble can be compared only to the famous souvenir that indifferently contains landmarks from all over the world, paying little attention to the probability of seeing them in a snowstorm. The *passage* as *boule de neige* (Figure 8.7) capable of shaking us between storefronts, theaters and bistros conveys the fact that commerce is the basis of this type of architecture, inside which the patrons trace fluctuating and placid trajectories, like snowflakes. This effect is made possible by the milky light from above, the use of iron for the structure and the shop windows, which were first imported from England.[20]

**FIGURE 8.7** *Boule de neige* of Paris © Antonello Boschi.

After all, in commerce the underpasses find a factor that evolves from its archetype, generating a hybrid capable of transforming the passerby into a customer, justifying greater investment in terms of construction. This is the moment in which the underpass tends to widen at the sides, to recreate the cross-section of a street in the above-ground world faced by timid storefronts: small businesses that have little in common with the sparkling display of goods in the ground-level gallerias, yet still represent an enlivening entropic factor.

What remains unvaried is the transitive character of the space, unlike the Parisian *passages* where the rising middle class, but also the less affluent classes, "qui n'aiment rien tant que jouir de leur propre spectacle. On s'y presse à la sortie des représentation théâtrales – beaucoup de passages couverts sont jumelés avec les salles – pour y être vu."[21]

The reservoir of potential new customers in the underground fabric continues to be prompted to enter these places only by obligatory transfers

**104** Sous passages

between transport lines, the possibility of saving time by shopping along these obligatory routes, or the chance for a respite from the chaotic traffic of the city.

This constant, which may or may not be considered a defect, can be observed from a dual vantage point. On the one hand, the spatial character that is the basis of the difference between these corridors, namely the equal and opposite sensations of lightness and weight they communicate; on the other, the new condition of the underpasses, which remains very distant from the variety of uses and fluxes contained in the sheltered galleries at ground level (Figure 8.8). Though on the surface one was inside a structure, the street was always nearby, and was a place in which stores and residences were seamlessly connected.[22]

As time passes the spatial device of the underpass has taken the path indicated by the dazzle of commerce[23] of a morphological evolution, without ever turning back. On a par with the explosion that has taken place in cities at all latitudes, with the resulting sprawl, we can state that the analogous clustering of underground pathways is a *fait accompli* in many contemporary cities. The route that originally simply connected A to B multiplies its terminal points in the more intricate developments – arriving

FIGURE 8.8  Stantec, Pedestrian undercrossing facility at Mariposa Land Port of Entry, Nogales (AZ) 2014 © 2021 Stantec Consulting Services Inc., All Rights Reserved.

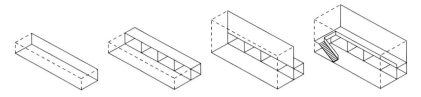

FIGURE 8.9 Flow patterns.

at notations for which all the letters of the alphabet would not suffice. To understand the resulting constellation, it is not enough to connect the dots as in a children's workbook; we have to also consider the upward development of these submerged works of architecture (Figure 8.9). Through the stratification of levels, a volume is reached that can be seen as comparable to the cross-section of a street. This segment-surface-volume transformation represents the best synthesis through which to understand the fact that these systems have always had a latent ambition, namely to effectively become parts of the city: a characteristic intrinsically sustained by the spatial concept with which Rudofsky associates the street,[24] i.e. not just the street surface, but also the entire volume including the surrounding frontage. Naturally there are no apartments on the first floor, and we are far from the *mixité* of the street level. Of course, the underpasses are not sunken *passages*, but the sounds that reach us from down there suggest the voices with which the street attracts its audience, shaping its movement,[25] and making it – after all – a true place.

## Notes

1. Walter Benjamin, *The Arcades Project* (Cambridge, MA: The Belknap Press, 1999), 9.
2. Anna Barbara, *Sensi, tempo e architettura: spazi possibili per umani e non* (Milan: Postmedia Books, 2012), 55.
3. A definition borrowed from the ranking Louis Kahn makes of spaces, subdividing them into directional, namely those with a prevailing direction, or non-directional, i.e. with a clear polarity that does not convey the idea of movement or crossing. In Louis I. Kahn, "The Room, The Street, The Human Agreement," *AIA Journal* 56 (September 1971): 33–34.
4. Marc Augé, "From Places to Non-Places," in *Non-Places: Introduction to an Anthropology of Supermodernity* (London: Verso, 1995), 75–115.
5. Koolhaas, *Delirious New York,* 100.
6. Benjamin, *The Arcades Project,* 417.
7. Michael Jakob, *The Bench in the Garden: An Inquiry into the Scopic History of a Bench* (Novato: Oro Editions, 2017).

**106** Sous passages

8 Robert Walser, *The Walk* (London: Serpent's Tail, 1992).
9 Neologism introduced by Foucault to identify real spaces but which represent a short circuit in relations with the surrounding spaces. Michel Foucault, *Utopies et hétérotopies*, recording of two France Culture radio conferences held on December 7 and 21, 1966.
10 Cf. Guy Debord, *The Society of The Spectacle* (New York: Zone Books, 1994).
11 Guy Debord, "Théorie de la dérive," *Les Lèvres nues* 9 (November 1956), 6–10.
12 Rem Koolhaas, "Junkspace," in *Project on the City 2* / Harvard Design School, *Guide to Shopping*, eds. Chuihua Judy Chung, Jeffrey Inaba, Rem Koolhaas, and Sze Tsung Leong, (Cologne: Taschen, 2001), 412.
13 Robert Venturi, Denise Scott Brown, and Steven Izenour, *Learning from Las Vegas. The Forgotten Symbolism of Architectural Form* (Cambridge, MA: MIT Press, 1972).
14 Code name that writers use to differ. *Tag bombing* is the reproduction of the own *tag* on a large scale in a specific urban area.
15 *Clochard* (from the French *clocher* to wobble), *barboni*, homeless, all synonyms that in reality betray places, times and ways of life that are only apparently similar.
16 *Przejście podziemne*, directed by Krzysztof Kieślowski, Poland 1973.
17 Jane Jacobs, *The Death and Life of Great American Cities* (New York: Vintage Books, 1961), 29–54.
18 Filippo La Porta, "Nuovi passages. Benjamin e la città contemporanea," *Scienze del Territorio* 3 (2015): 40.
19 Massimo Valentinotti, "Traversing the Darkness. A Contemporary View of a Mith," in *Passages: Dialogues with the Dark*, eds. Massimo Valentinotti, Armando De Zambotti, and Walter Bonaventura, (Milan: Mimesis, 2006), 103.
20 Giandomenico Amendola, *La città Postmoderna: magie e paure della metropoli contemporanea*, (Rome: Laterza, 2010), 127.
21 Jean-Claude Delorme, Anne-Marie Dubois, *Passages couverts parisiens* (Paris: Parigramme, 2002), 19–20.
22 Vanni Codeluppi, *Lo spettacolo della merce: i luoghi del consumo dai passages a Disney World*, (Milan: Bompiani, 2001), 48.
23 The reference is to the consumer society theorized by the French philosopher and sociologist. Jean Baudrillard, *The Consumer Society: Myths and Structures* (Thousand Oaks, CA: Sage, 1970).
24 Bernard Rudofsky, *Streets for People: A Primer for Americans* (New York: Van Nostrand Reinhold, 1969), 20.
25 Richard Sennett, *Building and Dwelling: Ethics for the City* (London: Penguin, 2018), 226–227.

# 9
# BURIED HIGH-RISES

When James Graham Ballard published one of his most famous novels – *High-Rise* (Figure 9.1)[1] – the *Unité d'Habitation* of Marseille had been in use for twenty-five years. The span of an entire generation was an ample one for an assessment of that collective experience in the light of at least two different perspectives. On the one hand, this period represents the cyclical evolution of a hypothetical family, which could have moved into one of the famous duplexes of the complex already in 1952 and had a child, now of

**FIGURE 9.1** Still taken from *High-Rise*, by Ben Wheatley, Great Britain 2015.

DOI: 10.4324/9781003214960-9

**FIGURE 9.2** Le Corbusier, view of the flat roof of the *Unité d'Habitation*, against the background of the Calanques, Marseille 1946–1952 © Antonio Salvi.

adult age and able to move away to live elsewhere. A scenario that brings to mind what Joseph Rykwert noticed during a visit to the roof of the *Maison du Fada*, where the children of the nursery school on the upper level had made drawings of their idea of a house (Figure 9.2).[2] Only some of the drawings made reference to the forms of that big complex on the outskirts of the city, while many others reverted to the archetypal scheme with a door, two windows and a nice red pitched roof.

On the other hand, the urban sphere also evolves parallel to the adaptation of the social sphere, and around the imposing earthbound Trans-Atlantic of the *Unité* we see not the open sea hypothesized by the architect, but an array of boats, large and small, worthy of a Mediterranean cove in midsummer.

> La nature a été reprise en considération. La ville, au lieu de devenir un pierrier impitoyable, est un grand parc. L'agglomération urbaine (est) traitée en ville verte. Soleil, espace, verdure. Les immeubles sont

posés dans la ville derrière la dentelle d'arbres. Le pacte est signé avec la nature.[3]

In this paraphrase-collage of the urban thinking of the architect provided by Choay, the nature that was envisioned as surrounding the building was instead polluted by other buildings, which in the best cases are bad copies of the original, and generally destroyed the myth of concentrating people in a single place in order to liberate the surroundings from the impact of man. In a photograph dated 1949 we see a pleased and patriotic Le Corbusier (Figure 9.3), flanked by a French flag lifted by the wind to take on a sculptural pose that might remind us – with less physical potency, but certainly with the same inner drive – of *Liberty Leading the People*, painted by Delacroix in 1830 (Figure 9.4). This curious dualism reminds us that the ardent climate of a people recouping the ideals of the French Revolution was not so different from the view that could be seen from the roof of the building (even without *citoyens*). A theory that finally crystallized as

**FIGURE 9.3** Le Corbusier and the flag raised above the *Unité d'habitation*, October 6, 1949 © FLC.

**FIGURE 9.4** Eugène Delacroix, *Liberty Leading the People*, 1830 © RMN – Grand Palais (Musée du Louvre) / Michel Urtado.

*architecture or revolution*, a provocative vision advanced by Le Corbusier, in favor of the first, though at a distance of thirty years.[4]

Nevertheless, the myth of the Minoan city-palace which the project set out to revive was fading, and the Parc National de Calanques – visible in the distance from the upper level – underscored the fact that the constructed island of the *Unitè* had to be seen as part of an artificial archipelago more similar to the speculative *Palm Islands* in Dubay than to the palace at Knossos in Crete.

The frenzy and drama of the housing emergency that was the most politically outstanding topic of modern architecture had by then been shifted out of the spotlight of debate in those years. The idea itself of being able to govern urban growth in an absolute and orderly way had already for some time begun to move towards the marked entropy of the diluted city, riding the wave of widespread affluence and industrial development after World War II.

To get back to the question of collective habitation, in 1975 Ballard – with the lucidity only madness can bring to the fore – describes the shock

Buried high-rises **111**

of a society in which "in a sense, these people were the vanguard of a well-to-do and well-educated proletariat of the future, boxed up in these expensive apartments with their elegant furniture and intelligent sensibilities, and no possibility to escape."[5] Undoubtedly, the condition of the writer took its cue from an idea of a pyramid of social stratification, in which the architect was at the top, father and custodian of his eschatological vision made of concrete and glass.

In this period the ferment of the radical movements had already begun in London, Tokyo and Florence, generating dozens of more or less all-encompassing utopian cities: the Instant City, Walking City and Plug-In City of *Archigram*, the Twelve Ideal Cities and Continuous Monument of *Superstudio*, and the endless cellular aggregation of the Metabolism movement. Most of these abstractions, supported by enticing graphics and collages, made no attempt to be credible and feasible like the project by Le Corbusier, and their makers willingly remained inside the cultural circles in which they enjoyed immediate fame, taking advantage of the exuberant climate of those years, the period of so-called "power to the imagination." All this contained, in essence, the concept of the large building disguised as a city, with turnkey solutions to the problem of housing, often forgetting all about the human scale and inevitably doing violence to that of the landscape. On the other side of the Atlantic the city hypothesized by Wright[6] – though it contained the famous mile-high skyscraper – was based on extensive land use, making the automobile into a simulacrum of freedom and democracy. But the boundless American plains were a luxury unavailable to little old Europe. Organic architecture too, much earlier than the radical examples, had exhausted its former thrust, leaving along the way many seeds but few truly fruitful results.

What if all these dwellings, these parts of the city, were instead sunken into the ground, like craters below the horizon line? What would happen were we to deprive everyone of the view of the Calanques, while at the same time preventing them from imposing views on each other?

Crossing the organic scenario with that of radical design, a starting point emerges from which to generate the activity of Paolo Soleri, an Italian who had settled in the United States, and a disciple of Wright by vocation. The communitarian idealizations produced starting at the end of the 1950s rotated around the theoretical concept of *arcology*, proposed as a syncretic combination of architecture and ecology. The principle suggested the idea of bringing together high residential density and an inner ecology of the design, something that today would have a lot to do with the concepts of the circular economy. Among the proposals a strong bond with the earth

## 112  Buried high-rises

emerged, above all in the hypotheses indicated as Stonebow and Novanoah I. These experiments were structured on territories of variable morphology, like canyons and gorges, exploiting the altitude variations of the terrain to embrace the ground and reach the light. In spite of the presence of these level shifts, Soleri began with one premise:

> since the surface of the earth is a two-dimensional configuration, the natural landscape is not the appropriate frame for the complex life of society. As a result, man must create a metropolitan landscape in his own image. It should not be a tenuous film of organic material, but an energetic lump that is physically compact, dense and multilevel; it should be a solid of three compatible dimensions.[7]

The clustering of these anthill-like phalansteries – just two of the many examples formulated during the architect's career – had the objective of a return to the earth, but with the ultimate goal of creating gigantic self-sufficient organisms that would discreetly appear on the horizon, inserting themselves as punctiform episodes capable of encompassing an entire city. Soleri's research managed to take on concrete form only in partial and relatively small cases (Figures 9.5 and 9.6),[8] an outcome that is quite predictable considering the scale of intervention implied by his projects. An even more extreme perspective, if possible, was the one imagined by Oscar Newman, treating the underground scenario as the alter ego of the Manhattan that has been built atop the earth's surface (Figure 9.7). This suggestion was undoubtedly prompted by fear of nuclear conflict, in the middle of the Cold War: a city as bunker – to be excavated, perhaps with intentional sarcasm, precisely through atomic explosions – which would have spelled survival for all of New York City. The inverted copy would be connected to its original through vertical access systems and was entirely organized inside a sphere that would also reproduce the vault of the heavens. As in *The Truman Show*, the new metropolitan alternative would have relied on a painstaking illusion of reality as we know it, in order to make the residents feel at ease, as if nothing had changed. Approaching Newman's provocative proposal with the proper respect, it is possible to underscore one of the main problems that must inevitably be faced by underground collective architecture: the relationship with light. After all, it is not by chance that the ideal world described by Ballard – the communal residence of a perfect society equipped with all the comforts – is thrown into crisis by a series of small blackouts. Using this narrative ploy, the author introduces darkness as a factor that breaks down inhibitions, allowing the inhabitants to indulge their worst instincts, releasing their repressed and hidden frustrations.

Buried high-rises **113**

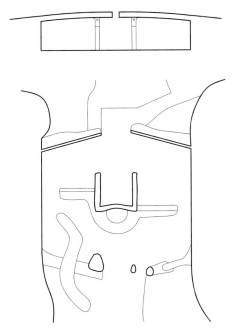

**FIGURE 9.5** Paolo Soleri, plan and section of the Earth House, Cosanti 1956.

**FIGURE 9.6** Paolo Soleri, standing outside the Earth House, which is partly underground, Cosanti, Paradise Valley (AZ) 1959 © Leonard Mc-Combe / Time& Life Pictures / Getty Image.

**114** Buried high-rises

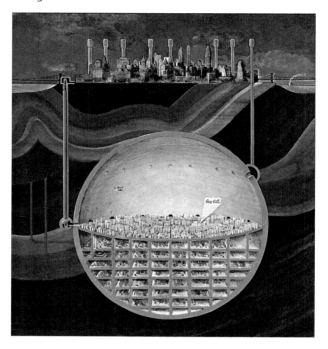

**FIGURE 9.7**  Oscar Newman, *Underground City Beneath Manhattan*, *Esquire* (1 December 1969): 187 © Esquire.

Even for a great spellbinder like Le Corbusier, it was hard to convince people that the *Rue Intérieure*, the intestinal access route of the *Unité* totally without natural light, was an architectural device developed to emphasize by contrast the great luminosity of the lodgings to which it led. Even a well-devised machine like that of Marseille had to have its shadow zones, which remain in the uterus of the great vessel.

Taking this work of architecture as a compositional paradigm of communal dwelling, we can try to suggest a proposal in which excavation becomes the starting point through which the archetype of the *condominium* fulfills the destiny implied by its etymological meaning.[9] By extension of this two-sided form of control-respect of others, we can imagine sinking the *Unité d'Habitation* into a flared hole capable of containing it. This "burial" implies above all erasing it from the horizon, not only returning nature to its original profile but also preventing the interception of the sun's rays that would cast shadows on the adjacent lots. A large excavation, a subtraction capable of containing the building in question and permitting

## Buried high-rises 115

the entry of the light required by the residences. An abyss that plunges down to a depth of fifty meters, with a cross-section that forms an isosceles trapezoid where one base is the double of the other.[10] This container – which could be defined as a suitable cellar in which to store the *bottle rack* of Le Corbusier – would emerge over ground level only with the roof of the building, like the tip of an iceberg that shows itself at polar latitudes. And precisely the roof – with the exception of the public thoroughfare of the seventh and eighth floors – was the place of concentration of the communal space atop the ideal building containing a village envisioned by the architect. The nursery school, the gymnasium, a solarium, an outdoor auditorium and a fitness trail of about 300 meters thus return to street level, after a long period of exile up in the sky. As a result, the access to the apartments would be from above, through the two lines of contact between the city and the building, namely those of the north and south sides. But this is not the only one of the five points for a new architecture to be resemanticized. The pilotis, the powerful legs that previously functioned as a means through which the inhabited volume was raised above the street, lose this task, but they could certainly become – in case of persistent precipitation – a spatial device capable of keeping the entire organism dry and in good health. With another small effort of the imagination, and the rise of water at the foot of the construction, the powerful, evocative image of the ship resurfaces, that of the earthbound Trans-Atlantic liner that has finally found its own little sea.

It might seem superfluous to emphasize that this enormous excavation would be a daunting feat on various fronts, starting with costs and including technical dynamics and the adaptation of the inhabitants. While still today for a child a drawing of a house cannot be imagined as a standard condo, it would be even less plausible for kids to envision a return to the bowels of the earth. Though sunlight for the apartments placed on an east-west axis would be ensured by the flared shape of the hole, the view from the units would resemble not the coveted sight of the Calanques in the distance, but the sensation of suddenly finding oneself in a rocky ravine. The compromise in terms of outlook is necessary to exempt the edges from the view of themselves, and to be able to rethink them as large green areas comparable to natural horizons, outside the perimeters of cities. The inhabited landscape would wind up resembling a wheel of Swiss cheese, and the footprint of the outskirts could be seen as a histological sample of different tissues whose gaps would contain the pathways. Different tissues corresponding to different projects, which starting from the example of the *Unité souterrain* (Figure 9.8) would share only the constant of the excavation

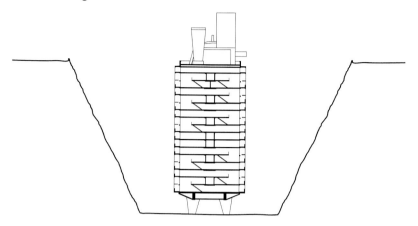

**FIGURE 9.8** Section of the *Unité d'Habitation souterrain*.

**FIGURE 9.9** Sandro Botticelli, *Abyss of Hell*, 1480–1495 © Biblioteca Apostolica Vaticana.

of a burrow, in this case drastically reducing the impact of a bad design with respect to the context. While Alberti spoke of a "house like [...] some small city" and of a "house as a miniature city,"[11] and paraphrasing the famous description of Urbino by Baldassarre Castiglione of "a city in

Buried high-rises **117**

the form of a palace,"[12] here the image that emerges is that of a territorial pattern of Dantean circles (Figure 9.9), capable of restoring the constructed area to the realm of delights worthy of a Garden of Eden.

## Notes

1 James Graham Ballard, *High-Rise* (London: Jonathan Cape, 1975).
2 Joseph Rykwert, "In Search of a Lost House," *The Architectural Review* 1421 (July 2015): 24–27.
3 Françoise Choay, *L'urbanisme, utopies et réalités: une anthologie* (Paris: Seuil, 1965), 243.
   "Nature has once more been taken into consideration. The city, rather than becoming a merciless heap of stones, is a large park. The urban agglomeration [is] seen as a green city. Sunlight, space, greenery. The buildings are located in the city behind the lace of trees. The pact with nature is signed."
4 *Vers une architecture* was first published in 1923.
5 Ballard, *High-Rise*, 97.
6 The reference is to Broadacre City, whose low housing density would have allowed people to isolate themselves in the greenery and agriculture. Every housing lot included a plot of land of minimum 4000 sqm.
7 Paolo Soleri, "Conversation with the author, Palermo, November 25 and 30, 1999," in Antonietta Iolanda Lima, *Soleri: Architecture as Human Ecology* (New York: The Monacelli Press, 2003), 211.
8 Consider the projects of Cosanti and Arcosanti, carried on with great determination and inhabited by the architect himself from 1956 until his death in 2013. The worksite photograph showing Soleri with a bathing suit, shovel and dog is intriguing if we compare to the images of Le Corbusier, which are so crowded with workers.
9 From Latin *con*, together, and *dominium*, control.
10 Considering a width of twenty-four meters for the building, the excavation would measure forty-eight meters at the base and ninety-six meters at ground level.
11 Leon Battista Alberti, *On the Art of Building in Ten Books*, book I, chap. IV and book V, chap. XIV (Cambridge, MA: MIT Press, 1988), 23, 140.
12 Baldassarre Castiglione, *The Book of the Courtier* (New York: Frederick Ungar Publishing, 1959), 3.

# 10
## BRIGHTENING THE DARK
*Antonello Boschi and Antonio Salvi*

"In the pursuit of perfection in their works, some added and took away, as do those who work in wax, plaster, or clay, whom we call modelers. Some others began by only taking away, and by removing that material which is deemed superfluous, they sculpt; revealing in the marble a form, or the potential shape of man, which was at first concealed. There were Sculptors."[1] While the resemblance between sculpture and architecture had been outlined by Alberti in the first of his treatises and definitively sanctioned by Michelangelo in the famous letter to Benedetto Varchi,[2] the reference to underground architecture, to excavation as the founding action of a house, a building, a city, is less immediate. What is taken away from the sand, the earth and the rock is therefore a creation of spaces or, indeed, a removal, subtraction, working in negative terms.

Passing below ground level makes it possible to invert the meaning of construction and to make the variables of the above-ground world that govern architecture vanish into temporary absence. Thinking inside a chthonic environment translates into a *tabula rasa* with nothing to raze to the ground, replaced by a precise intention to erode that ground, acting as an infinite generator of places, doing without a corresponding quantity of horizons. There is no view of the outside to distract us from the volume in which we stand, no relationship of continuity beyond the cross-section we inhabit: at best we have glimpses, scraps, segments of sky that gather pure light. A use of light that has an even greater importance here with respect to that of the "surface," but one that cannot be grasped *sic et simpliciter* as a controllable, accountable quantity. This is not the achievement

DOI: 10.4324/9781003214960-10

Brightening the dark **119**

of a physical comfort urged by studies that gravitate around the measurable parameters of light sources: no preferable temperature (meaning color), no luminous flow (lumens) suited to an envisioned function, no surface on which to measure the resulting level of luminance (lux).

All this brings out the arbitrary and evocative character of these settings of invention, and the fact that the problems of architecture are generally not solved on a technical level.[3] In other words, the focus is on the atmosphere of the space, something that alerts the field of perception, also underlined "in everyday language [when] we speak of a 'change of atmosphere' denoting a qualitative change in which *quantity* of light is of only secondary importance."[4] Starting with this observation, we can reconsider the value of light in design to the point of the total reversal of its hierarchy: *architectura sine luce nulla architectura est.*[5] Light is therefore an inevitable reality, like gravity,[6] and at the same time the only one capable of overcoming it. Hence, we can approach it from the opposite position, under the ground, in which the "inevitable" condition with which to come to terms is total darkness. To paraphrase the precepts of Abbé Dinouart, author of *L'art de se taire*, we can state that the abysses of darkness are preferable to the overexposure to light that has had an impact on homes and workplaces, streets and squares, entire cities.

And

> it follows from these observations that to produce a sad, sombre impression, it is necessary to try to present, as I did in my funerary monuments, an architectural skeleton through the use of an absolutely bare wall and to convey an impression of buried architecture by using only low, sagging proportions buried in the earth; and, finally, by using light absorbing materials, to create a black image of an architecture of shadows outlined by even darker shadows.[7]

This quote is not here to indicate that an atmosphere, to be incisive, has to necessarily be melancholy or gloomy; the aim is to emphasize the fact that in the dichotomy staged between tragedy and comedy we are somehow forced to choose the former. Architecture all too often finds itself with its back to the wall of the "positivism" that is implicit in the public exercise of the craft. A world of images, of projects represented in overexposed and ethereal photographs, overflowing with light and inhabited by human cutout figures that recite their lines, communicating an eternal, inevitable, glossy sense of happiness.

The path we are attempting to track down does not pursue functions that justify the project, like the pretexts Boullée enacts in the form of

## 120 Antonello Boschi and Antonio Salvi

libraries, cenotaphs and palaces. The search is instead for the mere relationship between the individual, other human beings and space, hinting at but one distinction referring to the public or private nature of the work. No function pursued with form, meaning a story summed up in an image, the image of an atmosphere that alters depending on the eyes of the beholder, because "in certain situations, it is even more difficult not to imagine than to imagine in the first place."[8] An imagination, nevertheless, that is not left to chance, because although the observer can interpret it through an unavoidably subjective standpoint, the construction of the vague and the indeterminate requires particular caution: "a highly exact and meticulous attention to the composition of each image, to the minute definitions of details, to the choice of objects, to the lighting and the atmosphere, all in order to attain the desired degree of vagueness."[9]

The surrounding system of conditions in which to operate can therefore be summed up in a triple abstraction: place, comfort and function. The objective remains that of superimposing the emotional space of human nature on the *genius loci*, and the idea of passing from imminent to immanent needs on comfort, while keeping at a proper distance an exact function that could limit the image to a cycle of actions rather than reflections. The use of images becomes a theme capable of simultaneously opening up two separate aspects. On the one hand, the charm of photography seen as the rendering of a project reminds us of the concept of photographic portraiture raised by Barthes with respect to the multiple imaginaries that meet inside it. "In front of the lens, I am at the same time: the one I think I am, the one I want others to think I am, the one the photographer thinks I am, and the one he makes use of to exhibit his art."[10] By replacing the person with the project, we get closer to the idea that representing it in the direction of photorealism has a lot to do with this multifaceted understanding. The second aspect involves the degree of truthfulness that we are able – or wish – to communicate through the images produced. In this sense, we can observe a substantial evolution: "with photography, in the process of pictorial reproduction the hand was for the first time relieved of the principal artistic responsibilities, which henceforth lay with the eye alone as it peered into lens."[11] The construction of the virtual image, though generated through the laws of optics, overturns the dynamic of the process from photographing something depicted to depicting something photographed.

What, if not photography used as drawing, can manage to precisely transcribe the materials – light and space – with which we intend to work? This consideration takes on greater vigor if we consider the well-known analog process (secularized, at this point) in which the positive – the photograph – was revealed from the negative – the plate. This not only required darkness

Brightening the dark **121**

to make it possible to *develop* the visible, but also in most cases remained in darkness for the rest of its life, constantly awaiting reproduction. In the end, "the empty words of light are spoken in utter silence,"[12] which is definitively the best if not the only invariant of photography.

We began these reflections by hinting at the difference between architecture as a whole and underground architecture, and a similar difference emerges between external light, which according to Le Corbusier, as we know, produces the masterly play of objects brought into the light, and internal light, which "gives life to the spaces enclosed by the volume itself."[13] A difference that translates into a light that wants to embrace everything and is therefore indistinguishable from the construction, and a light that is directed at specific points, illuminating the darkness in which the structure is immersed in a differentiated way. Hence, the subterranean world reveals how a completely dark environment can take on life, vibrate and become space even simply due to the effects of a lit candle. In the end, the utterly new approach of photography introduced in cinema by John Alcott in *Barry Lyndon* is the offspring of the glimmering light of torches, oil lamps, candles that brightened Baroque rooms, first in Italy with Caravaggio and then in Europe with Gerard van Honthorst (Figure 10.1) and Georges de La Tour.

**FIGURE 10.1** Gerard van Honthorst, *Childhood of Christ*, 1620 Photograph © The State Hermitage Museum

The effects of light in a space full of impressions but without artificial lighting can change remarkably depending on the type of opening, the position, the direction, and the method – direct or indirect. The effect that comes closest to the presence of a traditional window in an excavated space is that of the cave of the Sibyl of Cumae, where a series of openings were cut into the tuff stone to guide the steps towards the chamber in which the future was told, according to legend. A light that arrives, then, from the side, reminding us of Hopper's preparatory studies for *Sun in an Empty Room* from 1963, when the American master precisely outlined the shadows cast inside the room, alternating brightly lit portions with dark vertical surfaces. Although Hopper claimed to not care particularly about his drawings,[14] the artist's ledgers offer the perfect calligraphic transcription of his idea of lateral light.

Of course, our example has a monumental scale (Figures 10.2 and 10.3) quite different from the domestic scale of Hopper's boxes – with the small figure in the rendering to remind us of this fact – but the dramatic effect

**FIGURE 10.2** Antonello Boschi, Antonio Salvi, view of *Room 1 with lateral light*, 2020.

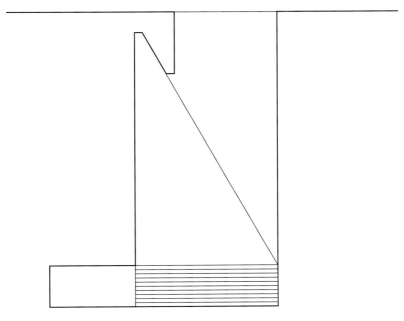

**FIGURE 10.3** Antonello Boschi, Antonio Salvi, section of *Room 1 with lateral light*, 2020.

of the almost Piranesian light, the accentuation of the contrasts and the rhythm are the same. A lateral, horizontal light that has seldom in history been transformed into vertical, and has rarely taken on "the liquid solemnity of the meridian daylight."[15]

In the past the only building lit from above was the Pantheon, precisely because only the gods could afford an opening nine meters in diameter that besides the light allowed rain, wind, cold and snow to pass through. Hence, the importance of underground buildings, which would not be impacted by these atmospheric nuisances. First of all, then, the water cisterns like the *Piscina Mirabilis*, almost a secular cathedral with its naves and cruciform pillars, whose name refers to the openings through which it was lighted for visitors on the Grand Tour.[16] This was an exception, since these spaces were usually completely without light, as demonstrated by the *Yerebatan Sarayı* – the "sunken palace" – of Istanbul, and have counterparts in the modern era in the tanks that supply water for our cities, admirably photographed by Peter Seidel when they have been emptied for maintenance work. While the effect could be compared to the solstice at the

Temple of Ptah at Karnak, when an ancestral light penetrates from a shaft and illuminates depending on the angle of the sunlight, a extended hand, a seated person or a statue, perhaps the building that evokes it best is the Danteum by Terragni, especially in the part that references the beginning of the Divine Comedy, with the hundred pillars to simulate a dark forest and the successive halls of hell, purgatory and above all paradise, with the invention of the glass columns.

Here the effect is not only multiplied, but also guided through conduits that add rhythm to the room and convey haloes of light down to the ground. A sort of organ of many pipes that transforms the darkness of the ceiling into a progressive radiance, conveyed by reflections off the floor and, in succession, the weaker reflections from the walls (Figures 10.4 and 10.5). A space of contemplation in which the lights have a theatrical effect, like so many spotlights that focus attention on the environment but also make it possible to isolate oneself, to listen, to meditate in a timeless

**FIGURE 10.4** Antonello Boschi, Antonio Salvi, view of *Room 2 with vertical light*, 2020.

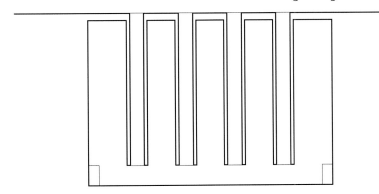

**FIGURE 10.5** Antonello Boschi, Antonio Salvi, section of *Room 2 with vertical light*, 2020.

place. In the hall we are therefore presented with a mediation between opaque pilasters and pilasters of light, where the stone grants substance to the verses of the poem "absence, / a more acute presence."[17] Access is from two doors at the sides of the space, precisely to replicate the effect of wonder felt when passing from a small room into another of great height: everything is introverted, gathered inward, silence. It is a type of vertical light we rarely come across in painting, precisely because it is a room *of invention,* but a painting like *Christ and the Woman Taken in Adultery* by Rembrandt can convey an idea of the effect this radiance can produce on people.

We spoke of the Pantheon, and there are those who have hypothesized that this work of architecture, once sunken into the ground, would be no more and no less than a grotto with a hole at the center.[18] One characteristic of the Roman oculus is that the sunlight roams along the walls, and when there is dust, smoke or mist in the air it shapes cones of light. The situation we have attempted to reproduce is different, when the space is not circular, the opening itself is not circular and above all the light is not at the center, but placed on one side of the box of the walls (Figures 10.6 and 10.7). This shift of axis, depending on the angle of the sunlight, makes it become oblique and brings out all the irregularities, joints and textures of the material it grazes, or illuminates the setting at the center of the underground room. We are indeed looking at a sort of cubic Pantheon, but one in which the light is distributed in a very different way than in its Hadrianic ancestor. The study by the sculptor Eduardo Chillida for Mount

**FIGURE 10.6** Antonello Boschi, Antonio Salvi, view of *Room 3 with diagonal light*, 2020.

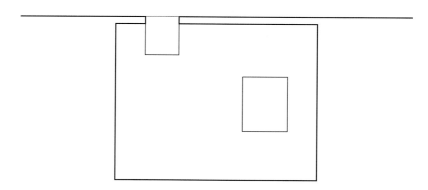

**FIGURE 10.7** Antonello Boschi, Antonio Salvi, section of *Room 3 with diagonal light*, 2020.

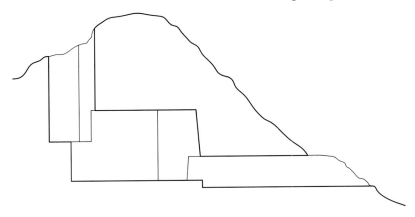

**FIGURE 10.8** Eduardo Chillida, section of the Mount Tyndaya's project, Fuerteventura 1996.

Tyndaya in the Canary Islands (Figure 10.8), with its sides of fifty meters and two large corner openings, is the best demonstration of how it is possible to create a work of sculpture-architecture that is absolutely invisible from the outside, where the flow of time is conveyed by the variations of brightness and darkness, sunlight and moonlight.[19] Our example too is a gigantic hollow, empty, subtracted space, but the opening astride the horizontal and the vertical gives rise to a diagonal beam that brightens the ceiling, which would otherwise always remain in darkness.

Other ways of lighting underground space also exist, which are actually variations on the approaches described thus far. First of all, the light from above that from a point becomes a line, forming a cut (Figures 10.9 and 10.10) that depending on the site, the changing seasons and hours can be limited to the projection of its profile on the ground, or can reach into the space with very marked angles. The Parisian atelier painted in the mid-1800s by Ary Johannes Lamme shows us the mechanism of lighting with the lateral part optionally darkened, and an open strip inserted in the roof (Figure 10.11). A skylight that, in turn, can become a chimney of light, completes with its mouth. The part that would theoretically receive less light is dominated by a diffused glow that again works by means of a fissure, driven down to the ground by a vertical wall.

If the light is too strong and causes glare and increased temperature, various types of screening can be used. Of course, it is possible to use

**FIGURE 10.9** Antonello Boschi, Antonio Salvi, view of *Room 4 with linear light*, 2020.

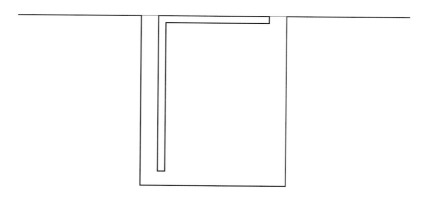

**FIGURE 10.10** Antonello Boschi, Antonio Salvi, section of *Room 4 with linear light*, 2020.

**FIGURE 10.11**   Ary Johannes Lamme, *Atelier d'Ary Scheffer, rue Chaptal*, 1851.

curtains, shutters and blinds that interact with the window, but when the openings are large the need arises to introduce a *brise-soleil* or sunscreen system (Figures 10.12 and 10.13). Apart from the prophet of this shading mechanism, namely Le Corbusier, the most vivid example is undoubtedly the Nordic Pavilion by Sverre Fehn at the Venice Biennale in 1962: a crossed array of partitions with a thickness of a few centimeters that produces an effect of diffused light that is always different, never banal. As in the *Adoration of the Shepherds* by Tintoretto (Figure 10.14) – where a two-story stable with widely placed roof beams, without a roof, allows light to penetrate and emphasize the presence of volumes and people – also in our example differently lighted zones are obtained, but without the clarity of direct lighting.

Perhaps it is precisely these gradual passages between light and darkness, with all the shadings, intermediate degrees and tones shadow can produce, that conveys the meaning of a place that finds shelter in the earth. The reference points of sun and moon are lacking except during particular

**FIGURE 10.12** Antonello Boschi, Antonio Salvi, view of *Room 5 with suffused light*, 2020.

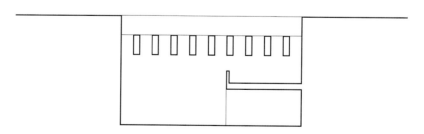

**FIGURE 10.13** Antonello Boschi, Antonio Salvi, section of *Room 5 with suffused light*, 2020.

moments of the day, but the vivid sensation remains of something primordial, an inner environment, a "distinct world of shadows. […] How many echoes, and what an impression, in that dimness!"[20]

Brightening the dark **131**

**FIGURE 10.14** Tintoretto, *The Adoration of the Shepherds*, 1578–1581 © Property of Scuola Grande di San Rocco in Venice.

## Notes

1. Leon Battista Alberti, *On Sculpture*, ed. Jason Arkles (n.p.: Lulu.com, 2013), 10.
2. Michelangelo Buonarroti, "To messer Benedetto Varchi," in *Life, Letters, and Poetry* (New York: Oxford University Press, 1999), 120. "I mean sculpture work which is fashioned to dint of taking away."
3. Alvar Aalto, "Euroopan jälleenrakentaminen tuo pinnalle aikamme rakennustaiteen keskeisimmän probleemin," *Arkkitehti* 5 (1941), quoted in English in Aarno Ruusuvuori, and Juhani Pallasmaa, eds. *Alvar Aalto 1898–1976* (Helsinki: Museum of Finnish Architecture, 1978), 113–114. "The problem of architecture cannot usually be solved at all using technical methods."
4. Pierre von Meiss, *Elements of Architecture: From Form to Place* (London: Routledge, 2011), 121.
5. Alberto Campo Baeza, "Intorno alla luce," *Domus* 760 (May 1994): 86–87.
6. Ibid., 86.
7. Étienne-Louis Boullée, *Architecture. Essay on Art*, part of Ms Français 9153 Bibliotèque National de Paris in Helen Rosenau, ed., *Boullées Treatise on Architecture* (London: Tiranti, 1967), 90.
8. Edward S. Casey, *Imagining: a Phenomenological Study* (Bloomington: Indiana University Press, 1976), 4.

## 132 Antonello Boschi and Antonio Salvi

9 Italo Calvino, *Six Memos for the Next Millennium* (Cambridge, MA: Harvard University Press, 1988), 59–60.

10 Roland Barthes, *Camera Lucida: Reflections on Photography* (New York: Hill and Wang, 1981), 13.

11 Walter Benjamin, *The Work of Art in the Age of Mechanical Reproduction* (London: Penguin, 2008), 4.

12 Steven Holl, *Parallax* (Basel: Birkhäuser, 2000), 104.

13 Franco Purini, *Comporre l'architettura* (Rome: Laterza, 2000), 114.

14 Gail Levin, *Edward Hopper: An Intimate Biography* (New York: Alfred A. Knopf, 1995), 251.

15 Roberto Longhi, *Piero della Francesca* (London: Frederick Warne, 1930), 32.

16 In the past the vaults had small openings that made it possible to gather water through the use of ropes and buckets. With time and neglect, these hatches grew wider, becoming openings that still bring light to these places today.

17 Attilio Bertolucci, *Sirio* (Parma: Minardi, 1929), 35.

18 Pierre Zoelly, *Terratektur. Einstieg in die unterirdische Architektur* (Basel: Birkhäuser, 1989), 123.

19 See Eduardo Chillida, *Lo spazio e il limite. Scritti e conversazioni sull'arte*, ed. Stefano Esengrini (Milan: Marinotti, 2010).

20 Jun'ichirō Tanizaki, *In Praise of Shadows* (New Haven, CT: Leete's Island Books, 1977), 26, 30.

# BIBLIOGRAPHY

Abdulak, Samir, and Pierre Pinon. "Maisons en pays islamique." *L'Architecture d'aujourd'hui* 167 (May–June 1973): 6–14.

Al-Temeemi, Ali A., and Doug J. Harris. "A Guideline for Assessing the Suitability of Earth-Sheltered Mass-Housing in Hot-Arid Climates." *Energy and Buildings* 36 (March 2004): 251–260.

Alberti, Leon Battista. *On Sculpture*, ed. Jason Arkles. n.p.: Lulu.com, 2013.

———. *On the Art of Building in Ten Books*. Cambridge, MA: MIT Press, 1988.

Amendola, Giandomenico. *La città Postmoderna: magie e paure della metropoli contemporanea*. Rome: Laterza, 2010.

Andreoli, Vittorino. *Fuga dal mondo*. Milan: Rizzoli, 2009.

Anselm, Akubue Jideofor. "Earth Shelters. A Review of Energy Conservation Properties in Earth Sheltered Housing." In *Energy Conservation*, ed. Azni Zain Ahmed, 125–148. Rijeka: In tec, 2012.

———. "Passive Annual Heat Storage Principles in Earth Sheltered Housing, a Supplementary Energy Saving System in Residential Housing." *Energy and Buildings* 40 (July 2008): 1214–1219.

Arecchi, Alberto. *La casa nella roccia. Architetture scavate e scolpite*. Milan: Mimesis, 2001.

Augé, Marc. *In the Metro*. Minneapolis: University of Minnesota Press, 2002.

———. "La complessità del sottosuolo." *La Repubblica*, October 20, 2006.

———. *Non-Places: Introduction to an Anthropology of Supermodernity*. London: Verso, 1995.

Avanza, Federica, Stefano Calchi Novati, and Simone De Munari. *Progettare il sottosuolo: elementi di cultura tecnica per l'architettura sotterranea*. Milan: FrancoAngeli, 1991.

Bachelard, Gaston. *The Poetics of Space*. Boston, MA: Beacon Press, 1969.

## 134 Bibliography

Baggs, Sydney A. "A Taxonomy of Underground Space." In *Proceedings of the Earth Sheltered Housing Conference and Exhibition*, 189–197. Minneapolis: University of Minnesota, 1980.

———. "The dugout Dwellings of an Outback Opal Mining Town in Australia." In *Underground Utilization: A Reference Manual of Selected Works*, ed. Truman Stauffer, 573–599. Kansas City: University of Missouri, 1978.

———. "Underground Earth-Insulated Architecture." *Building Economist* 16 (June 1977): 16–18.

Ballard, James Graham. *High-Rise*. London: Jonathan Cape, 1975.

Barbara, Anna. *Sensi, tempo e architettura: spazi possibili per umani e non*. Milan: Postmedia Books, 2012.

Barnard, John E. "A New Life – Underground." *Wentworth Institute Bulletin* 8 (October 1973): 8–10.

———. ed. *Ecology House*, undated brochure.

Barthes, Roland. *Camera Lucida: Reflections on Photography*. New York: Hill and Wang, 1981.

Baudrillard, Jean. *The Consumer Society: Myths and Structures*. Thousand Oaks, CA: Sage, 1970.

Behrens, Roy R. "Architecture, Art and Camouflage. L'origine militare del camouflage ad opera di un gruppo di artisti dell'esercito americano." *Lotus* 126 (November 2005): 75–83.

Bélanger, Pierre. "Underground Landscape: The Urbanism and Infrastructure of Toronto's Downtown Pedestrian Network." *Tunneling and Underground Space Technology* 22 (October 2006): 272–292.

Benjamin, Walter. *The Arcades Project*, ed. Rolf Tiedemann. Cambridge, MA: Belknap Press, 1999.

———. *The Work of Art in the Age of Mechanical Reproduction*. London: Penguin, 2008.

Bertolucci, Attilio. *Sirio*. Parma: Minardi, 1929.

Betsky, Aaron. *Landscrapers: Building with the Land*. London: Thames & Hudson, 2002.

Boeri, Stefano. "Bosco Verticale." *Area* 122 (May–June 2012): 102–111.

Borasi, Giovanna, and Mirko Zardini, eds. *Sorry, Out of Gas: Architecture's Response to the 1973 Oil Crisis*. Montréal-Mantova: Canadian Centre for Architecture-Corraini, 2007.

Borchia, Rosetta, and Olivia Nesci. *The Invisible Landscape: Discovering the Real Landscapes of Piero della Francesca*. Ancona: Il lavoro editoriale, 2012.

Borges, Jorge Luis. *Selected Poems*, ed. Alexander Coleman. New York: Penguin, 2000.

Boschi, Antonello. "La piccola città invisibile." *Rassegna* 87 (June 2007): 80–89.

Boschi, Antonello, and Andrea Bulleri. *Suture(s)*. Pisa: Pacini, 2011.

Boschi, Antonello, and Giorgio Croatto. *Filosofia del nascosto: costruire, pensare, abitare nel sottosuolo*. Venezia: Marsilio, 2015.

Bugatti, Angelo. *Progettare il sottosuolo nella città densa e nel paesaggio*, ed. Ioanni Delsante. Santarcangelo di Romagna: Maggioli, 2010.

## Bibliography **135**

Buonarroti, Michelangelo. *Life, Letters, and Poetry.* New York: Oxford University Press, 1999.

Burkhardt, François, and Paul Virilio. "Abbiamo bisogno del sottosuolo." *Domus* 879 (March 2005): 108–111.

———. "Tutto è architettura. François Burkhardt intervista Hans Hollein." *Rassegna* 87 (June 2007): 22–29.

Calvino, Italo. *Invisible Cities.* New York: Harcourt Brace Jovanovich, 1974.

———. *Six Memos for the Next Millennium.* Cambridge, MA: Harvard University Press, 1988.

———. *The Complete Cosmicomics.* Boston, MA and New York: Houghton Mifflin Harcourt Jonathan, 2014.

Campo Baeza, Alberto. "Intorno alla luce." *Domus* 760 (May 1994): 86–87.

Carmody, John, and Raymond L. Sterling. *Underground Space Design. A Guide to Subsurface Utilization and Design for People in Underground Spaces.* New York: Van Nostrand Reinhold, 1993.

Carotenuto, Aldo. *I sotterranei dell'anima. Tra i mostri della follia e gli dèi della creazione.* Milan: Bompiani, 2008.

Carrol, Lewis. *Alice's Adventures in Wonderland.* Boston, MA: Lee and Shepard, 1869.

Casarin, Chiara, and Davide Fornari, eds. *Estetiche del camouflage.* Milan: et al./ edizioni, 2010.

Casey, Edward S. *Imagining: a Phenomenological Study.* Bloomington: Indiana University Press, 1976.

Castiglione, Baldassarre. *The Book of the Courtier.* New York: Frederick Ungar Publishing, 1959.

Castiglioni, Piero. "Compiti visivi e riflessi psicologici dell'illuminazione artificiale." In *Proceedings of the Conference La Città Sotterranea nell'Area Metropolitana,* 83–84. Milan: Sindacato regionale ingegneri liberi professionisti della Lombardia, 1987.

Cattaneo, Carlo. *Alcuni* scritti. Milan: Bonomi e Scotti, 1846.

Chillida, Eduardo. *Lo spazio e il limite. Scritti e conversazioni sull'arte,* ed. Stefano Esengrini. Milan: Marinotti, 2010.

Choay, Françoise. *L'urbanisme, utopies et réalités: une anthologie.* Paris: Seuil, 1965.

Chung, Chuihua Judy, Jeffrey Inaba, Rem Koolhaas, and Sze Tsung. Leong, eds. *Project on the City 2* / Harvard Design School, *Guide to Shopping.* Cologne: Taschen, 2001.

Clément, Gilles. *Manifeste du Tiers paysage.* Paris: Sujet-objet éd, 2004.

Codeluppi, Vanni. *Lo spettacolo della merce: i luoghi del consumo dai passages a Disney World.* Milan: Bompiani, 2001.

Commerson, Jean-Louis-Auguste. *Pensées d'un emballeur: pour faire suite aux Maximes de La Rochefoucauld.* Paris: Martinon, 1851.

Coogan, Alan H. "Classification and Valuation of Subsurface Space." *Underground Space* 4 (1979): 175–186.

Cronin, Archibald Joseph. *The Stars Look Down.* Boston, MA: Little, Brown and company, 1963.

## 136 Bibliography

Debord, Guy. "Théorie de la derive." *Les Lèvres nues* 9 (November 1956): 6–10.

———. *The Society of The Spectacle*. New York: Zone Books, 1994.

de Botton, Alain. *The Architecture of Happiness*. London, Penguin, 2007.

Dickens, Charles. *Hard Times. For These Times*. Cambridge, MA: Riverside Press, 1869.

Edelhart, Mike. "The Food Life Underground." *Omni* 4 (January 1980): 50–55, 92.

Freud, Sigmund. *Civilization and its Discontents*. Mineola, NY: Dover Publications 1994.

Furrer, Bernhard. "Unterirdische Bauten im Historischen Bereich-Ein Grundsatzpapier der Eidgenössischen Kommision für Denkemalpflege." *Nike Bulletin* 4 (December 2001): 11–16.

Gabriella Vanotti, and Claudia Perassi, eds. *In limine. Ricerche su marginalità e periferia nel mondo antico*. Milan: V&P università, 2004.

Gibelli, Maria Cristina, and Edoardo Salzano, eds. *No Sprawl: perché è necessario controllare la dispersione urbana e il consumo di suolo*. Firenze: Alinea, 2006.

Ginsburg, Leslie B. "Summing Up." *Architectural Review* 154 (August 1973): 263–266.

Giuffrè, Maria, Paola Barbera, and Gabriella Cianciolo Cosentino, eds. *The Time of Schinkel and the Age of Neoclassicism between Palermo and Berlin*. Cannitello, RC: Biblioteca del Cenide, 2006.

Goethe, Johann Wolfang. *Wilhelm Meister's Years of Apprenticeship*. Richmond: Alma Classics, 2013.

Golany, Gideon. *Earth-Sheltered Habitat: History, Architecture and Urban Design*. New York: Van Nostrand Reinhold, 1983.

Golany, Gideon, and Toshio Ojima. *Geo-Space Urban Design*. New York: Wiley & Sons, 1996.

Gomez-Moriana, Rafael. "Il mascheramento quotidiano nella città. Il paradosso dell'occultamento per assimilazione con il contesto urbano." *Lotus* 126 (December 2005): 126–137.

Hait, John N. *Passive Annual Heat Storage: Improving the Design of Earth Shelters, Or, How to Store Summer's Sunshine to Keep Your Wigwam Warm All Winter*. Missoula, MT: Rocky Mountain Research Center, 1983.

Heidegger, Martin. *Building Dwelling Thinking*. New York: Harper Colophon Books, 1971.

Hershorn, Shel, Dimitri Kessel, Francis Miller, Ralph Morse, and Eric Schall, eds. "Fallout Shelters. You Could Be among the 97% to Survive If You Follow on These Pages… How to Build Shelters… Where to Hide in Cities… What to Do during an Attack." *Life* 11 (September 15, 1961): 95–108.

Holberg, Ludvig. *A Journey to the World Under-Ground*. London: T. Astley and B. Collins, 1742.

Holl, Steven. *Parallax*. Basel: Birkhäuser, 2000.

Horsbrugh, Patrick. "Urban Geotecture: The Invisible Features of the Civic Profile." In *Proceedings of the Conference on Alternatives in Energy Conservation: The Use of Earth Covered Buildings*, ed. Frank L. Moreland, 152–153. Fort Worth, TX: National Science Foundation, 1975.

# Bibliography 137

Hughey, Joseph, and Robert Tye. "Psychological Reactions to Working Underground: A Study of Attitudes, Beliefs and Evaluations." *Underground Space* 5–6 (1983): 381–386.

Ingersoll, Richard. *Sprawltown. Looking for the City on Its Edges.* New York: Princeton Architectural Press, 2006.

Jacobs, Jane. *The Death and Life of Great American Cities.* New York: Vintage Books, 1961.

Jakob, Michael. *Le paysage.* Gollion: Infolio editions, 2008.

———. *The Bench in the Garden: An Inquiry into the Scopic History of a Bench.* Novato: Oro Editions, 2017.

Jean-Claude Delorme, Anne-Marie Dubois. *Passages couverts parisiens.* Paris: Parigramme, 2002.

Jones, Stephen. *The History of Poland: From Its Origin as a Nation to the Commencement of the Year 1795. To Which Is Prefixed an Accurate Account of the Geography and Government of That Country and the Customs and Manners of Its Inhabitants.* London: Vernor & Hood, 1795.

Jung, Carl Gustav. *Modern Man in Search of a Soul.* London: Routledge, 2001.

———. *The Earth Has a Soul: The Nature Writings of C.G. Jung,* ed. Meredith Sabini. Berkeley, CA: North Atlantic Books, 2002.

Kahn, Louis I. "The Room, The Street, The Human Agreement." *AIA Journal* 56 (September 1971): 33–34.

Kempe, David. *Living Underground. A History of Cave and Cliff Dwelling.* London: The Herbert Press, 1988.

Kent, Richard. "The Role of Mystery in Preferences for Shopping Malls." *Landscape Journal* 1 (March 1989): 28–35.

Koenig, Giovanni Klaus. "Immersi nel terreno." *Ottagono* 74 (September 1984): 18–23.

Koolhaas, Rem. *Delirious New York: A Retroactive Manifesto for Manhattan.* New York: Oxford University Press, 1978.

Labs, Kenneth. "The Architectural Underground." *Underground Space* 1 (May–June 1976): 1–8, 135–156.

LaNier, Royce. *Geotecture.* Paris: University of Notre Dame, 1970.

Lanouette, William J. "Architect Sinks to New Depths and Digs It." *Chicago Tribune,* February 8, 1975.

La Porta, Filippo. "Nuovi passages. Benjamin e la città contemporanea." *Scienze del Territorio* 3 (2015): 38–43.

Leach, Neil. *Camouflage.* Cambridge, MA: MIT Press, 2006.

Le Corbusier. *Precisions on the Present State of Architecture and City Planning: with an American prologue, a Brazilian corollary followed by The temperature of Paris and The atmosphere of Moscow.* Cambridge, MA: MIT Press, 1991.

———. *Towards a New Architecture.* Mineola, NY: Dover, 1986.

Lee, Kaiman, ed. *Encyclopedia of Energy-Efficient Building Design: 391 Practical Case Studies.* Boston, MA: Environmental Design and Research Center, 1977.

Lesser, Wendy. *The Life below the Ground. A Study of the Subterranean in Literature and History.* Winchester, MA: Faber & Faber, 1987.

**138** Bibliography

Lethaby, William R. *Architecture, Mysticism and Myth*. New York: Dover, 1891.

Levin, Gail. *Edward Hopper: An Intimate Biography*. New York: Alfred A. Knopf, 1995.

Lima, Antonietta Iolanda. *Soleri: Architecture as Human Ecology*. New York: The Monacelli Press, 2003.

Longhi, Roberto. *Piero della Francesca*. London: Frederick Warne, 1930.

Loubes, Jean-Paul. *Archi troglo*. Roquevaire: Parenthèses, 1984.

Matsumoto, Naoji, Eiji Koyanagi, and Sigeyuki Seta. "Physical and Mental Factors of Anticipation in the Streetscape." In *Proceedings of the International Conference on Environment-Behaviour Studies for the 21th Century*, 283–286. Tokyo: 1997.

Maupassant, Guy de. *La Vie Errante and Others Stories*. New York: J.H. Sears & Company Inc., 1922.

Merleau-Ponty, Maurice. *The Visible and the Invisible: Followed by Working Notes*, ed. Claude Lefort. Evanston, IL: Northwestern University Press, 1968.

Micara, Ludovico. s.v. "Scavare/Colmare." In *Manuale. Forme insediative e infrastrutture*, ed. Aimaro Oreglia D'Isola, 306–308. Venezia: Aimaro, 2002.

Montalbini, Maurizio. "Stazioni ipogee. Esperimenti per un habitat possibile." *Rassegna* 87 (June 2007): 126–133.

Mulazzani, Marco. "Werner Tscholl, Casa SMRS & A, Castelbello, Bolzano." *Casabella* 886, (June 2018): 16–29, 102.

Mumford, Lewis. *The City in History. Its Origins, Its Transformations and Its Prospects*. New York: Harcourt, Brace & World, 1961.

Neumann, Dietrich, ed. *Film Architecture: Set Designs from Metropolis to Blade Runner*. Munich: Prestel, 1996.

Nicoletti, Manfredi. *L'architettura delle caverne*. Rome: Laterza, 1980.

O.M.A., Rem Koolhaas, and Bruce Mau. *S, M, L, XL: Small, Medium, Large, Extra-Large*, ed. Jennifer Sigler. New York: The Monacelli Press, 1995.

Oppewal, Harmen, and Harry Timmermans. "Modeling Consumer Perception of Public Space in Shopping Centers." *Environment and Behavior* 31 (January 1999): 45–65.

Philipp, Klaus Jan. *Karl Friedrich Schinkel, Späte Projekte Late projects*. 2 vols. Stuttgart and London: Axel Menges, 2000.

Philips, Patricia, and James Wines. *The Highrise of Homes / Site*. New York: Rizzoli, 1982.

Polano, Sergio. "L'architettura della sottrazione." *Casabella* 659 (June 1998): 2.

Purini, Franco. *Comporre l'architettura*. Rome: Laterza, 2000.

Rosenau, Helen, ed. *Boullées Treatise on Architecture*. London: Tiranti, 1967.

Rossi, Aldo. *The Architecture of the City*. Cambridge, MA: MIT Press, 1982.

Rudofsky, Bernard. *Streets for People: A Primer for Americans*. New York: Van Nostrand Reinhold, 1969.

———. *The Prodigious Builders: Notes Toward a Natural History of Architecture with Special Regard to those Species that are Traditionally Neglected or Downright Ignored*. New York: Harcourt Brace Jovanovich, 1977.

Ruusuvuori, Aarno, and Juhani Pallasmaa, eds. *Alvar Aalto 1898–1976*. Helsinki: Museum of Finnish Architecture, 1978.

## Bibliography 139

Rykwert, Joseph. "In Search of a Lost House." *The Architectural Review* 1421 (July 2015): 24–27.

"Saving by Going Underground." *AIA Journal* 61 (February 1974): 48–49.

Scheerbart, Paul. Letter to Bruno Taut dated February 10, 1914, then in "Glasshausbriefe." *Frühlicht* 3 (February 1920): 45–48.

Scheibach, Michael. *Atomic Narratives and American Youth: Coming of Age with the Atom, 1945–1955.* Jefferson, NC and London: McFarland & Company, 2003.

Schinkel, Karl Friedrich. *Viaggio in Sicilia*, eds. Michele Cometa, and Gottfried Riemann. Messina: Sicania, 1990.

Sennett, Richard. *Building and Dwelling: Ethics for the City.* London: Penguin, 2018.

Settis, Salvatore. *Paesaggio costituzione cemento. La battaglia per l'ambiente contro il degrado civile.*: Einaudi, 2010.

Smay, V. Elaine. "Underground Houses-Low Fuel Bills, Low Maintenance, Privacy, Security." *Popular Science* 4 (April 1977): 84–89, 155.

Spiegel, Walter F. "Air Quality and Heat Transfer." *The Use of Earth Covered Buildings.* In *Proceedings of the Conference Alternatives in Energy Conservation*, ed. Frank L. Moreland, 247–256. Fort Worth, TX: National Science Foundation, 1975.

Stein, Gertrude. *Picasso.* London: B. T. Batsford, 1938.

———. *The Autobiography of Alice B. Toklas.* New York: The Literary Guild, 1933.

Steiner, Dietmar. "Subarchitecture: Interview with Hans Hollein." *Domus* 812 (February 1999): 4–6.

Tanizaki, Jun'ichirō. *In Praise of Shadows.* New Haven, CT: Leete's Island Books, 1977.

Tempesta, Tiziano. *Alla ricerca del paesaggio palladiano. Un'indagine sul paesaggio delle ville venete in età contemporanea.* Legnaro: University of Padova, 2015.

Tosco, Carlo. *Il paesaggio come storia.* Bologna: il Mulino, 2007.

Trabucco, Francesco. "La fabbrica dei fiori. Un progetto di Marco Zanuso per l'area del Vallone San Rocco a Napoli, 1988." *Rassegna* 87 (June 2007): 54–63.

Trinquesse, Yves. *Soleil en sous-sol.* Paris: Desforges, 1977.

Tscholl, Werner. "Hábitat Troglodita, House SMRS &A, Castelbello (Italy)." *Arquitectura Viva* 209 (November 2018): 32–35.

Turri, Eugenio. *Il paesaggio e il silenzio.* Venice: Marsilio, 2004.

Utudjian, Édouard. *Architecture et urbanisme souterrains.* Paris: Robert Laffont, 1966.

———. *L'urbanisme souterrain.* Paris: Presses Universitaires de France, 1964.

Valentinotti, Massimo, Armando De Zambotti, and Walter Bonaventura, eds. *Dialogues with the Dark.* Milan: Mimesis, 2006.

Van Dronkelaar, Chris, Daniel Cóstola, Ritzki A. Mangkuto, and Jan L.M. Hensen. "Heating and Cooling Energy Demand in Underground Buildings: Potential for Saving in Various Climates and Functions." *Energy and Buildings* 71 (December 2013): 129–136.

Venezia, Francesco. "Incidenti a reazione poetica." *Domus* 681 (March 1987): 46–48.

Venturi, Robert, Denise Scott Brown, and Steven Izenour. *Learning from Las Vegas. The Forgotten Symbolism of Architectural Form.* Cambridge, MA: MIT Press, 1972.

## 140 Bibliography

Vercelloni, Matteo. "Earth House, Gyeonggi-do, South Korea (Byoungsoo Cho and others)." *Casabella* 799 (March 2011): 27–30.

Verne, Jules. *Journey to the Centre of the Earth.* London: Puffin, 1994.

Vindum, Kjed. "Eine Höhle für Jorn / A Cave for Jorn." *Daidalos* 48 (June 1993): 62–67.

Virilio, Paul, *Art as Far as the Eye Can See.* Oxford: Berg, 2007.

von Frisch, Karl. *Animal Architecture.* New York: Harcourt Brace Jovanovich, 1974.

von Meiss, Pierre. *Elements of Architecture: From Form to Place.* London: Routledge, 2011.

Wada, Yuji, and Hinako Sakugawa. "Psychological Effects of Working Underground." *Tunnelling and Underground Space Technology* 1–2 (1990): 33–37.

Walser, Robert. *The Walk.* London: Serpent's Tail, 1992.

Warnock, Gavin J. "New Frontiers of Inner Space-Underground★." *Underground Space* 1 (1978): 1–7.

Wells, Herbert George. *The Time Machine.* New York: Henry Holt & Co., 1895.

Wells, Malcolm. *Gentle Architecture.* New York: McGraw-Hill, 1981.

———. *Underground Designs.* Andover, MA: Brick House, 1977.

Wordsworth, William. *The Poetical Works.* London: Longman, Rees, Orme, Brown & Green, 1827.

Xueyuan, Hou, and Yu Su. "The Urban Underground Space Environment and Human Performance." *Tunnelling and Underground Space Technology* 2 (1988): 193–200.

Yan, Huo. "The Effects of Cave Dwelling on Human Health." *Tunnelling and Underground Space Technology* 2 (1986): 171–175.

Ylinen, Jaakko. "Architectural Design, Spatial Planning." In *The Rock Engineering Alternative*, ed. Kari Saari, 77–88. Helsinki: Finnish Tunnelling Association, 1988.

Zacharias, John. "Choosing a Path in the Underground: Visual Information and Preference." In *Proceedings of the 9th International Conference ACUUS Urban Underground Space a Resource for Cities*, 1–9. Turin: ACUUS, 2002.

Zoelly, Pierre. *Terratektur: Einstieg in die unterirdische Architektur.* Basel: Birkhäuser, 1989.

# INDEX

Note: *Italic* page numbers refer to figures and page numbers followed by "n" denote endnotes.

Aalto, Alvar 131n3
Abdulak, Samir 66n18
Abildgaard, Nicolai 5, *86*
*Abyss oh Hell 116*
*The Adventures of Tom Sawyer* 27n15
*The Adoration of the Shepherds*
  129, *131*
Alberti, Leon Battista 116, 117n11, 118,
  131n1
Albini, Franco 12, *12*
Alcott, John 121
*Alice's Adventures in Wonderland* 42n22
*All the President's Men* 7
Al-Temeemi, Ali A. 79n14
Amendola, Giandomenico 106n20
Andreoli, Vittorino 13n4
Anselm, Akubue Jideofor 94n11–12
Appleton, Jay 24
*The Arcades Project* 105n1, 105n6
Archea Associati 52, *52, 53*
Archigram 111
architecture: ablative 40; above-ground
  33, 36; authenticity in 33; clandestine
  7; conservation 73; cryptal 4;
  Five Points of 43; lobotomy 97;
  mobile 4; organic 111; sculpture

127; spontaneous 30; superficial 9;
  temperature 84; troglodyte 60
arcology 111
Arcosanti 117n8
Arecchi, Alberto 14n6
artificial caverns 25
*Atelier d'Ary Scheffer, rue Chaptal 129*
*The Atomic Café* 67
*The Atomic City* 67, *68*
*Atomic Power* 67
atrium design 84
attic *22,* 23
Auer, Albrecht *90*
Augé, Marc 26n2, 27n3, 105n4
Avanza, Federica 14n20

Bachelard, Gaston 22, 27n14, 40,
  42n23, 100
Baggs, Sydney A. 59, 66n9, 78n9,
  94n3–5, 94n15–16
Ballard, James Graham 107, 110, 112,
  117n1, 117n5
Barbant, Charles 5
Barbara, Anna 105n2
Barnard, John E. 69, 70, *70,* 71, 73, 78,
  78n8–9, 78n11, 79n15, 83, 94n7

**142** Index

Barry, John 58
*Barry Lyndon* 121
Barthes, Roland 120, 132n10
basements 15, 17, 22, 23, 26
*Batman Returns* 5
Baudrillard, Jean 106n23
BCHO Architects *61, 73, 75*
Bearzot, Cinzia 41n1
*The Beginning or the End* 67
Behrens, Roy R. 55n21
Bélanger, Pierre 14n16
Benjamin, Walter 27n5, 95, 96, 102, 105n1, 105n6, 132n11
Bensemra, Zohra *57*
Benthem Crouwel Architects *96*
Bertolucci, Attilio 132n17
Betsky, Aaron 14n8, 42n18, 66n19
*Blast from the Past* 7, 69
Boeri, Stefano 41n14
Bong Joon-ho 5, *6*
Borasi, Giovanna 78n6
Borchia, Rosetta 55n17
Boret, Bertrand *30*
Borges, Jorge Luis 61, 66n15
Boschi, Antonello 14n11, 41n4, 55n22, 55n25, 65n3, *122–126, 128, 130*
Bosco Verticale (Vertical Forest) 34, 41n14
Botta, Mario 51, *52*
Botticelli, Sandro *116*
de Botton, Alain 54n8
*boule de neige* 102, *103*
Boullée, Étienne-Louis 36, *36,* 119, 131n7
Broux, Prosper *32*
building: basement level 22; character of 9; energy savings 83; mixed and hybrid 59; open-air 69; and tunnels 36; typology 43
Bulleri, Andrea 14n11
Burkhardt, François 41n15
Burns, Joseph *39*
burrows 102, 116
Burton, Tim 5

Calchi Novati, Stefano 14n20
Calvino, Italo 41n2–3, 77, 79n18, 79n20, 132n9
camouflage 29, 47, 49, *51,* 55n21, 60, 67, 75

Campo Baeza, Alberto 131n5–6
Cantina Antinori *52, 53*
Cantina Petra *52*
Caravaggio *53,* 121
Carmody, John 14n20, 27n17, 66n10
Carotenuto, Aldo 26n1
Carroll, Lewis 38, 42n22
Casanova, Giacomo 4
Casarin, Chiara 55n22
Casey, Edward S. 131n8
Castiglioni, Piero 66n14, 116, 117n12
*The Castle of Otranto* 4
Cattaneo, Carlo 55n19
cave-dwelling populations 77
caves: Cordari 21; Plato's 4; Sibyl's 11–12, 18, *18, 122*
cellar 7, 22–23, *23,* 26, 115
Cenotaph for Isaac Newton 36, *36*
Chanéac 40
*Chemin de fermétropolitain* 15, 17
*Childhood of Christ* 121
Chillida, Eduardo 125, *127*, 132n19
China 25–26, 59, 80, 83
Choay, Françoise 109, 117n3
*Christ and the Woman Taken in Adultery* 125
cinema 4, 35, 46, 47, 121
cladding 41n15, 49
Clemens, Johan Frederik *86*
Clément, Gilles 54n7
cliff house 60–62, *62*
climate 4, 22, 25, 32, 44, 62, 70, 71, 74, 75, 81, 83–85, 109, 111
Codeluppi, Vanni 106n22
*Commedia* 4
Commerson, Jean-Louis-Auguste 44, 54n5
*The Complete Cosmicomics* 79n18, 79n20
construction: aeronautical 41n15; echo of 7; evolution of 9; function of 83; human and animal 38; meaning of 32, 118; self 69; sub 33; subterranean 43; technologies 30; territories of 40; underground 7, 22, 32, 83; virtual image 120
Coober Pedy 81, *81,* 86
Coogan, Alan H. 65n6
Cook, Peter 40
*Cosanti 113,* 117n8

Cóstola, Daniel 66n17, 94n6, 94n8
Couronnes station 24
Cristina, Maria Luisa 27n6
Cronin, Archibald Joseph 21, 27n11
Cryptoporticus 1, *2*
Cumaean Sibyl 11
Cuyperspassage *96*
Cyrano de Bergerac 4

Dante 4, 17, *18*
*Dante and Virgil in Hell 18*
Dean, Loomis *68*
Debord, Guy 98, *99*, 106n10–11
Delacroix, Eugène *18*, 109, *110*
de La Tour, Georges 121
Delorme, Jan-Claude 106n21
De Munari, Simone 14n20
Depero, Fortunato 36
diachronic approach 96
Dickens, Charles 27n9
*Die operettenhafte Kulisse* 33
Dinouart, Abbé 119
*The diptych of the Dukes of Urbino* 48, *48*
Donne, John 65
Dostoevsky, Fyodor 15, *16*
van Dronkelaar, Chris 66n17, 94n6, 94n8
Dubois, Anne-Marie 106n21

Earth House *61, 73, 75, 113*
earth-sheltered house *60,* 60, 62
Eco-city 29
Ecology House 69, *70*
Edelhart, Mike 78n12
embankment 49, 59
Erskine, Ralph 40
*espacesindécis* 45
European Environmental Agency 44
excavation 26, 27n10, 30, 49, 63, 69, 75, 81, 83, 88, 90, 102, 114–115, 117n10, 118
*Existenzminimum* 102
*Extreme measures* 7

*façadism* 33, *34*
*fait accompli* 104
fallout shelters 17, *68*
Fanfani, Amintore 49
Fehn, Sverre 129

Fidone, Emanuele 42n16
*flâneur* 19, 97
flow patterns *105*
Ford, Simon 5
Fornari, Davide 55n22
Foucault, Michel 106n9
Four Corners 70
Freud, Sigmund 1, 13n3, 27n4
Furrer, Bernhard 41n7, 41n9
Future Systems *60*

Gabetti, Roberto & Aimaro Isola 38, *39*
Gaudí, Antoni 36
gazes 15, 17, 23, 98
Gibelli, Maria Cristina 54n6
Ginsburg, Leslie B. 54n9
Glass Farm 49, *50*
Goethe, Johann Wolfgang 54n13
Golany, Gideon S. 65n4, 65n7, 66n16, 78n9, 93n1, 94n13
Gómez-Moriana, Rafael 41n10
*Grattacieli e tunnel* 36
gray zone 45
grottos 9, 18, 21, 125
*Gulliver's Travels* 4
Gyeonggi-do 73

habitual design approach 46
Hait, John N. 94n11
*Hard Times. Four these Times* 27n9
Harris, Doug J. 79n14
Heidegger, Martin 32, 41n6
Hensen, Jan L.M. 66n17, 94n6, 94n8
Hershorn, Shel 78n7
*High-Rise* (Ballard) 107, 117n1, 117n5
*High-Rise* (Wheatley) *107*
Holberg, Ludvig 4, 94n14
*The Hole* 7
Holl, Steven 132n12
Hollein, Hans 27n10, 42n17
Homer 17
van Honthorst, Gerard 121, *121*
Hopper, Edward 122
Hopper, Jerry *68*
Horsbrugh, Patrick 65n5
housing: democratic 67; emergency 110; row 59, 63; typologies 59

**144** Index

Hughey, Joseph 27n19
Hugo, Victor 5

*The Incredulity of Saint Thomas 53*
Ingersoll, Richard 54n6
*In Praise of Shadows* 132n20
*interieur* 95
*Invisible Cities* 41n2–3
isometric 40, *74, 77*
Izenour, Steven 106n13

Jacobs, Jane 101, 106n17
Jakob, Michael 54n10, 105n7
Jerusalem 85
Jones, Stephen 10, 14n17
Jung, Carl Gustav 15, 14n19, 23, 28n22

Kahn, Louis I. 105n3
Kansas City 25, *25*
Kaplan, Stephen 24
Kaplan, Rachel 24
Kavanagh, Ros *50*
Kell Brothers *16*
Kempe, David 65n1, 78n10
Kennedy, John Fitzgerald 69, 78n3
Kent, Richard 27n16
Kessel, Dimitri 78n7
Kieślowski, Krysztof 101, *101,* 106n16
Kindersley, Dorling *38*
Kircher, Athanasius 4, *4*
Klim, Niels 4, 85, *86*
Koenig, Giovanni Klaus 14n21
Koolhaas, Rem 34, 41n8, 41n12, 105n5, 106n12
Koyanagi, Eiji 14n13

Labs, Kenneth B. 65n1, 65n5, 65n8, 78n9, 78n11
Lamme, Ary Johannes 127, *129*
landscape 7, 24, 45–47, *48,* 49, 54, 55n24, 67, 75, *81,* 86, 92, 95–97, 111–112, 115
landscrapers 36
Lane, Jack *70, 73*
Lang, Fritz 5, *6*
LaNier, Royce 65n5
Lanouette, William J. 79n16
La Porta, Filippo 106n18
*La Vie Errante and Others Stories* 55n14

Leach, Neil 55n22
Le Corbusier 43, 44, *44,* 54n2, 54n4, 55n20, *108,* 109, *109,* 110, 111, 114, 115, 117n8, 121, 129
Lee, Kaiman 78n8
Leonardo da Vinci *3*
Leschot, Georges *31*
*Les Indesnoires* 5
*Les Misérables* 5
Lesser, Wendy 13n5, 27n15
Lethaby, William R. 79n21
Levi, Primo 45
Levin, Gail 132n14
*Liberty Leading the People* 109, *110*
light 11, 13, 17, 20, 23, 24, 26, 27n8, 41n15, 60, 61, 69, 74, 75, 92, 98, 102, 107, 118–130; ancestral 124; artificial 102; effects of 122; external 121; horizontal 123; internal 121; lateral 122; mechanism of 127; natural 13, 19, 26, 114; quantity of 61; and space 102, 120; use of 118
Ligne Maginot 7
Linders, Jannes *96*
*The Line* 30
literature 4, 5, 19, 80
Longhi, Roberto 132n15
Lorenzo the Magnificent 18
Loubes, Jean-Paul 65n2
Lucas, George 58, *58*
Luke Skywalker 58, *58*
Lyutomskiy, Nikolay 29

Maggi, Moreno *8*
*Maison du Fada* 108
Malator House *60*
Mangkuto, Ritzki A. 66n17, 94n6, 94n8
Marinetti, Filippo Tommaso 49
Massin, Leonida 36
Matmata 56, *57,* 70, 83
Matsumoto, Naoji 14n13
Maupassant, Guy de 46, 55n14
McCombe, Leonard *113*
Merleau-Ponty, Maurice 54, 55n26
*Metropolis* 5, *6*
Metz, Don 73
Micara, Ludovico 55n18
Michelangelo Buonarroti 118, 131n2
Miler, Francis 78n7

## Index 145

*mimesis* 49
Mimetic House 49, *50*
*Modern Times* 98
Montalbini, Maurizio 19, 27n7
Morris, Christopher *24*
Morse, Ralph 78n7
Mulazzani, Marco 94n19
Mumford, Lewis 7, 14n10, 35
*Mundus subterraneus* 4
MVRDV *50*

Naked City 98, *99*
neologism 42n18, 106n9
Nesci, Olivia 55n17
Neumann, Dietrich 14n7
de Neuville, Alphonse *31*
Newman, Oscar 29, 112, *114*
Newton, Isaac 36, *36*
*Nicolai Klimii iter subterraneum* 4
Nicoletti, Manfredi 94n18
*A Nightmare on Elm Street* 7
Novanoah 40, 112

Ojima, Toshio 93n1
*One World or None* 67
Oppewal, Harmen 14n14
Orianda Palace 21
Orlando, Paolo 27n6

Pac-Man 98, *99*
PAHS 84
Pal, George *89*
panorama 46–47, 60, 77
Pantheon 123, 125
Paoli, Gino 79n19
*Parasite* 5, *6*
Passage Jouffroy *97*
passages 4–5, 7, 12, 20, 26, 29, 40, 49,
    56, 58, 59, 62, 78, 85, 90, 96–98,
    100–103, 105
passive cooling 75, 84
patio typology 84
pedestrian 1, 7, 40, 43, *104*
*Pedestrian Subway (Przejściepodziemne)*
    101, *101*, 106n16
Philips, Patricia 41n13
philosophy 26
photography 120–121
Piero della Francesca *48,* 48
Pinon, Pierre 66n18

Piranesi, Giovanni Battista 5, *20, 20*
*Piscina Mirabilis* 11, *11, 123*
*pissoirs* 101
pit house 60–61, *61, 70*
Plan Cerdá 63, *64*
play subway 17
Poe, Edgar Allan 4
Polano, Sergio 14n9
power to the imagination 111
Predock, Antoine 42n18
Pre-Mycenaean Crete 102
*Prepared Landscapes* 40
Purini, Franco 132n13

quarries 47

rabbit hole 38, *38*
Re, Luciano *39*
Réduit of the Swiss Alps 7
Reed, Carol 7
Rembrandt 125
Renzo Piano Building Workshop *8*
reverse archaeology 33
Riller, René *93*
Riou, Édouard *5*
Rocault, Jules *10*
roof-cellar dichotomy 22
rope hoists 10
Rosa, Asor 55n15
Rossi, Aldo 33, 41n11
Rudofsky, Bernard 13n2, 38, 42n20,
    105, 106n24
Ruskin, John 49
*Rue Intérieure* 114
Rykwert, Joseph 108, 117n2

Sakugawa, Hinako 28n21
Salgari, Emilio 80
Salvi, Antonio *122–126, 128, 130*
Salzano, Edoardo 54n6
Sanmenxia *63–64*
Sartini, Martina 27n6
Savorelli, Pietro *12, 53*
Schall, Eric 78n7
Scheerbart, Paul 10, 14n18
Scheibach, Michael 78n2, 78n4
Scherschel, Joseph *45*
Schinkel, Karl Friedrich 21, *21,*
    27n12–13
Schliemann, Heinrich 17

**146** Index

Scott Brown, Denise 106n13
SeARCH + CMA *62*
Seidel, Peter 123
semantic noise 13
semi-static thermal condition 82
Sennett, Richard 106n25
Seta, Sigeyuki 14n13
Settis, Salvatore 54n11
Shaw, Martin T. *81*
Sibyl of Cumae 122
Siffre, Michel 19
*Sirio* 132n17
Situationist movement 98
*Six Memos for the Next Millennium* 132n9
skyscraper 34, 36, 38, 43, 111
SLOAP 45, 54n9
slope design 84
Smay, Elaine V. 94n7
social gazes 17
Softroom Architects *39*
Solaria House *37*
Soleri, Paolo 40, 111–112, *113*, 117n7–8
*Someone to Watch Over Me* 7
*Soylent Green* 7
Spiegel, Walter F. 94n10
*The Spiral Staircase* 7
SRMS & A house 90, *90*
Stantec *104*
*The Stars Look Down* 27n11
*Star Wars* 58, *58*
steam-driven machine 21
Stein, Gertrude 55n21
Steiner, Dietmar 27n10
Sterling, Raymond L. 14n20, 59, 66n10
Stevens, Dominic *50*
Stonebow 112
Su, Yu 28n20, 94n9
*Subarctic Cities* 40
subgrade type 59
*Subtropolis 25*
suburban 8, *45,* 77
*Subway* 7
subway 9, 17, 40, *100*
Sullivan, Louis 84
*Sun in an Empty Room* 122
sunlight 11, 36, 60–62, 71, 102, 115, 117n3, 124, 125, 127

superficial projects 25
Superstudio, 111
Swayze, Jay 73
Swift, Jonathan 4
Swiss Federal Commission on Historic Monuments 33
Swiss Pavilion 43, *44*

tag bombing 100, *100,* 106n14
Talponia 38, *39*
Tanizaki, Jun'ichirō 132n20
telluric spirit 35
temperature 13, 13n1, 20, 25, 80–81, 83–85, 119, 127
Tempesta, Tiziano 54n12
Termite Pavilion 38, *39*
terraced villas 47
Terragni 124
terrain 23, 56, 59, 61, 67, 75, 77, 83–85, 112
*terrains artificiels* 49
*Terratektur* 75
territory 8, 34, 43, 55n24, 100, 101
thermoregulation 80–81
*Things to Come* 7
*The Third Man* 6
three-dimensional 38, 43, *64, 65*
*THX 1138* 7
*The Time Machine* (Pal) *89*
*The Time Machine* (Wells) 5
Timmermans, Harry 14n14
Tintoretto, Jacopo Robusti known as 129, *131*
*Toscana Felix* 46
Tosco, Carlo 55n24
Trabucco, Francesco 14n12
trapezoidal section *19*
Treasure Museum of San Lorenzo 12, *12*
Trinquesse, Yves 61, 66n13
*The Truman Show* 112
trust 23
Tscholl, Werner 90, *90,* 94n19
tunnels: branching 98; Cryptoporticus 1; effect 9; French 17; sloping 56; transport in 15, vehicular 7
Turri, Eugenio 55n23
Tuscan countryside 49
*Twelve Monkeys* 7
Tye, Robert 27n19

Index **147**

*Underground* 7
underground 1, 5, 7, 9, 10, 13, 15, 20, 22, 25, *25*, 26, 29, 30, 32, 35, *37*, 40, 42n25, 47, 58–61, *63*, 73, 78n84–86, 92n1, 95–98, 100, 103, 112, *113*, 118, 121, 125; approach 70; brethren 96; buildings 84, 123; construction 7, 22, 32, 83; courtyard 71, 74; dwelling 60, 83; housing 62, 71; International Style 75; London 15, 98; passages 101, 102; pathways 4, 98, 104; rail lines 1, 7; rail systems 23; residential buildings 83; shelter 67–68; spaces 1, 7, 19, 30, 36, 59, 80, 84, 127; utopia-reality dualism 47; volume types 84
*Underground City Beneath Manhattan* 114
*Unité d'Habitation* 107–108, *108 ,109,* 110, 114–115, *116*
United States 25, 60, 70, 78n1, 111
urban sprawl 44–45
utopia-reality dualism 47
Utudjian, Édouard 29, 41n5, 42n24–25, 43, 54n1

Valentinotti, Massimo 106n19
Varchi, Benedetto 118
vegetation 21, 35
Venetian villas 51
Venezia, Francesco 54n3
ventilation 5, 30, 81, 85, *87,* 88, *88, 89,* 90, 91
Venturi, Robert 100, 106n13
Vercelloni, Matteo 79n17
Verne, Jules 5, *5,* 14n22, 80, 86
Vilagudin, Graciela *2*
*Villes Cratères* 40
Vindum, Kjed 66n12
Virgil 17, *18*
Virilio, Paul 41n15
Visconti, Luchino 46
*Voyage au centre de la terre* 5, *5,* 13, 14n22
*Voyage dans la lune* 4
*Voyage in Sicily* 21, 27n12

von Frisch, Karl 42n21
von Meiss, Pierre 131n4
Vulcano Buono 8, *8*

Wada, Yuji 28n21
Walker, Alanson Burton 34, 41n12
Walpole, Horace 4
Walser, Robert 98, 106n8
Warnock, Gavin J. 65n6
*The Warriors* 7
Weir, Peter 112
wells 11, 49, 60, 88, 89, *89*
Wells, Herbert George 5, 88, 94n17
Wells, Malcolm 36, *37,* 42n19, 60, 66n11, 69, 73
Western Residential Unit *39*
Wheatley, Ben *107*
White Cliffs 81, *82*
Wieliczka salt mine 10, *10*
*Wilhelm Meister's Years of Apprenticeship* 54n13
Willis Faber & Dumas Headquarters 49
wind park *47*
Wines, James 34, *35,* 41n13
Winston House 73
Wooseop Hwang *75, 76*
Wordsworth, William 78, 79n22
World War II 17, 45, *51,* 67, 110
Wright, Frank Lloyd 111

Xueyuan, Hou 28n20, 94n9

Yan, Huo 93n2
*Yerebatan Sarayı* 123
Yoon Dong-joo 73
Ylinen, Jaakko 27n18

Zacharias, John 14n15
Zanuso, Marco 8
*Zapiskiizpodpol'ja* 15, *16*
Zardini, Mirco 78n6
*Zaziedans le metro* 7
zero shadow effect 13
Zoelly, Pier 132n18

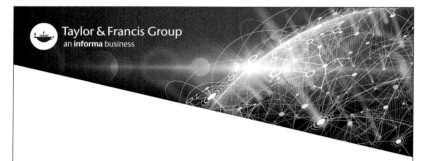